P9-ECL-296

The Kids' Fun-Filled Search & Find Fascinating Fact Book

By
Anthony Tallarico

3535 West Peterson Ave.
Chicago, IL 60659

Manufactured in the United States of America

STRANGE BUT TRUE MYSTERIES

Search and find lots of interesting facts about:

- The Giant Statues of Easter Island
- The Bermuda Triangle
- Loch Ness Monster
- Stonehenge
- Amelia Earhart
- King Tut's Curse
- Bigfoot
- Atlantis
- Another Jonah
- The Tunguska Explosion
- The Mary Celeste

THE GIANT STATUES OF EASTER ISLAND

On Easter Sunday, 1722, Dutch Admiral Jacob Roggeveen sailed to a small island in the South Pacific. When he went ashore he discovered more than 600 giant statues, some over 40 feet tall, carved from stone. In 1947, Thor Heyerdahl, a Norwegian archeologist, led an expedition to discover how the statues got there.

See if you can find all the things you did or didn't know about the Giant Statues of Easter Island in this picture. Don't forget to look for the following fun things, too.

- ☐ Artist
- ☐ Banana leaves
- ☐ Bone
- ☐ Broom
- ☐ Carrot
- ☐ Drum
- ☐ Duck
- ☐ Flower
- ☐ Flying bat
- ☐ Football
- ☐ Graduate
- ☐ Guitar
- ☐ Key
- ☐ Ladder
- ☐ Mouse
- ☐ Owl
- ☐ Paintbrush
- ☐ Painted eggs (3)
- ☐ Party hats (2)
- ☐ Pelican
- ☐ Periscope
- ☐ Photographer
- ☐ Ring
- ☐ Rocking chair
- ☐ Skateboard
- ☐ Stars (3)
- ☐ Telescope
- ☐ Toucan
- ☐ Truck
- ☐ Unicorn
- ☐ Wagon
- ☐ Water bucket
- ☐ Witch

What was used to carve the statues?
What was the name of Heyerdahl's raft?

EASTER ISLAND IS IN THE SOUTH PACIFIC, ABOUT 2,400 MILES FROM CHILE.
THE ISLAND IS GOVERNED BY CHILE.
IT'S A VOLCANIC ISLAND.
ADMIRAL ROGGEVEEN REACHED EASTER ISLAND ON EASTER SUNDAY, 1722.
THAT'S HOW IT GOT ITS NAME.
THIS ISLAND IS 63 SQUARE MILES AND HAS NO STREAMS RUNNING THROUGH IT.
ABOUT 1,600 PEOPLE LIVE ON THIS ISLAND, ALL IN THE VILLAGE OF *HANGA ROA*.
THE STATUES WERE CARVED USING STONE HAND PICKS.
THE STATUES ARE EYELESS.
THEY WERE MOVED ACROSS THE ISLAND.
WOW
DO NOT DISTURB.
I'M ON VACATION.
I'M LOOKING FOR MY CARROT!
I'M LOST!
PRESENT-DAY ISLANDERS BELIEVE THAT THEIR ANCESTORS THOUGHT THE STATUES HAD *SUPERNATURAL* POWERS.
WOODEN TABLETS WITH VERY STRANGE WRITING WERE ALSO FOUND ON EASTER ISLAND.
REALLY?
I DIDN'T KNOW THAT!
NO ONE HAS BEEN ABLE TO FIGURE OUT WHAT THE WRITING SAYS.
SOME SCIENTISTS THINK THAT EASTER ISLAND AND THE POLYNESIAN ISLANDS WERE SETTLED BY PEOPLE FROM ASIA WHO CREATED THESE STATUES.
ARCHEOLOGIST THOR HEYERDAHL, BELIEVED PEOPLE FROM ANCIENT PERU SAILED TO EASTER ISLAND AND TAUGHT THE ISLANDERS HOW TO CARVE THESE STATUES.
KON-TIKI IS A SUN GOD IN ANCIENT PERU. HE WAS SUPPOSED TO HAVE BEEN DRIVEN AWAY FROM PERU AND SAILED WESTWARD.
HEYERDAHL BUILT A RAFT TO PROVE IT WAS POSSIBLE TO SAIL FROM SOUTH AMERICA TO A POLYNESIAN ISLAND.
HE NAMED HIS RAFT *KON-TIKI*.
IT TOOK HIM 102 DAYS TO ARRIVE AT A POLYNESIAN ISLAND.
THE RAFT WAS MADE OF THE SAME MATERIALS KNOWN TO THE ANCIENT PERUVIANS.

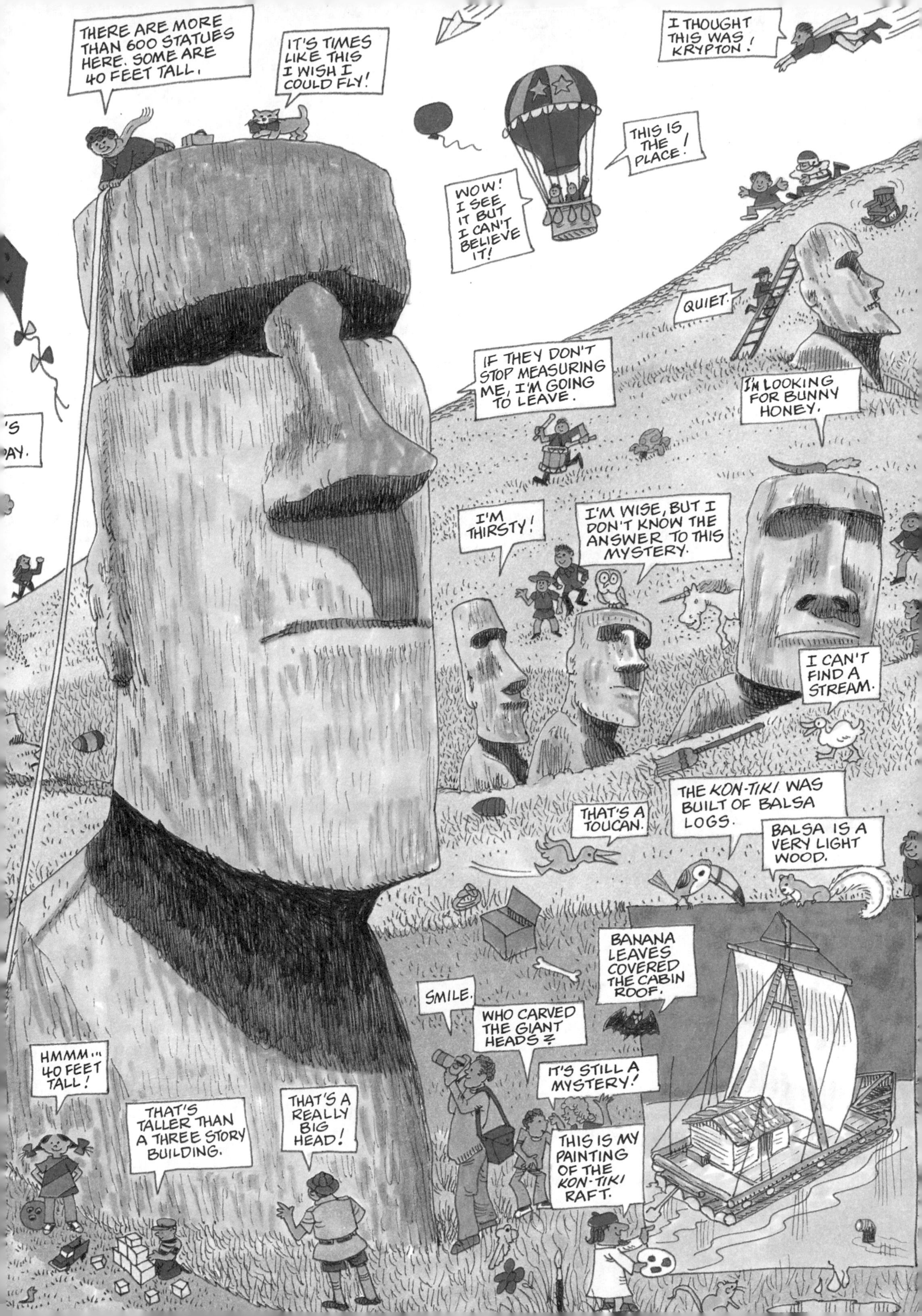

THERE ARE MORE THAN 600 STATUES HERE. SOME ARE 40 FEET TALL.
IT'S TIMES LIKE THIS I WISH I COULD FLY!
I THOUGHT THIS WAS KRYPTON!
THIS IS THE PLACE!
WOW! I SEE IT BUT I CAN'T BELIEVE IT!
QUIET.
IF THEY DON'T STOP MEASURING ME, I'M GOING TO LEAVE.
I'M LOOKING FOR BUNNY HONEY.
I'M THIRSTY!
I'M WISE, BUT I DON'T KNOW THE ANSWER TO THIS MYSTERY.
I CAN'T FIND A STREAM.
THE KON-TIKI WAS BUILT OF BALSA LOGS.
THAT'S A TOUCAN.
BALSA IS A VERY LIGHT WOOD.
BANANA LEAVES COVERED THE CABIN ROOF.
SMILE.
WHO CARVED THE GIANT HEADS?
IT'S STILL A MYSTERY!
HMMM... 40 FEET TALL!
THAT'S TALLER THAN A THREE STORY BUILDING.
THAT'S A REALLY BIG HEAD!
THIS IS MY PAINTING OF THE KON-TIKI RAFT.

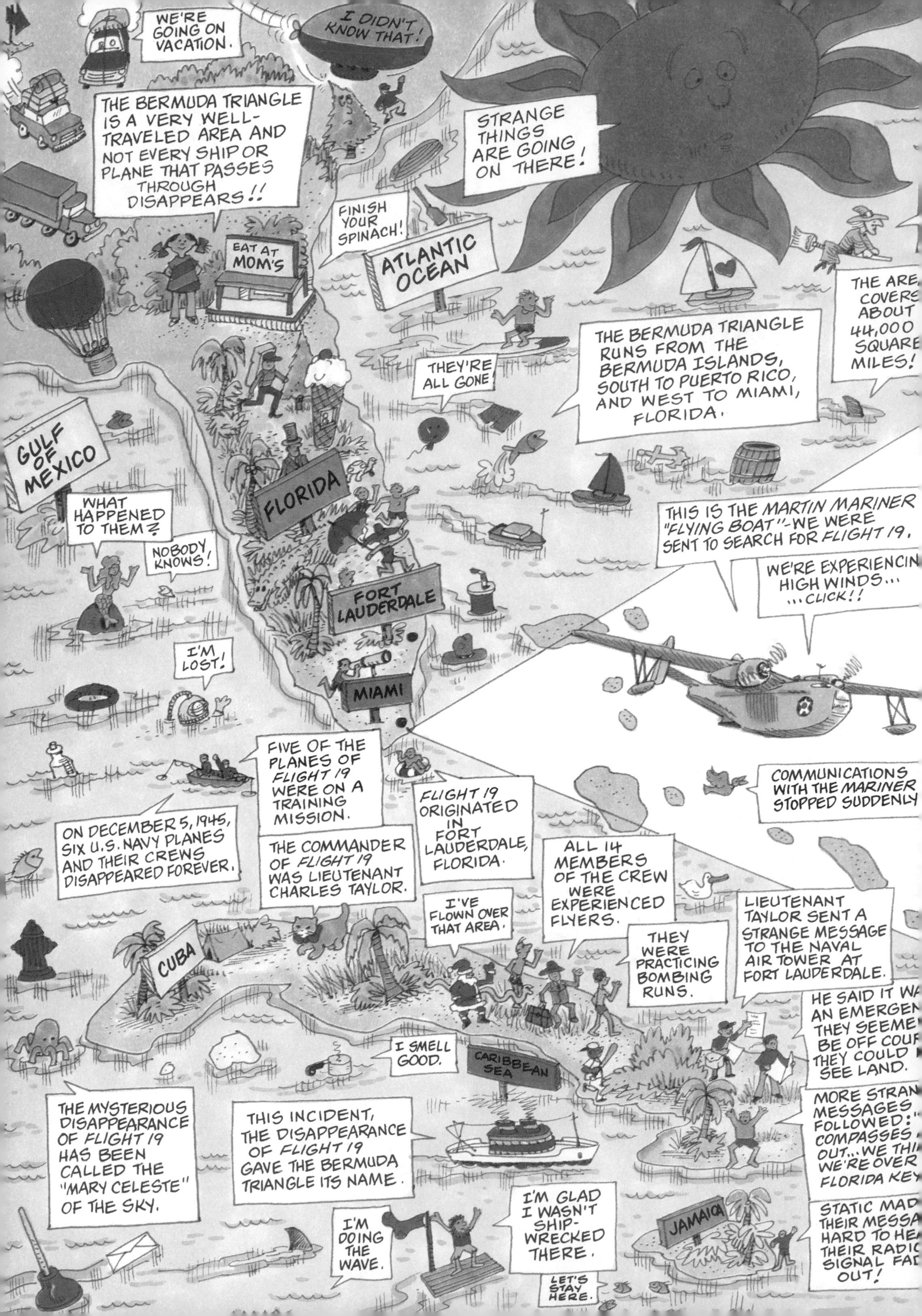
WE'RE GOING ON VACATION.
I DIDN'T KNOW THAT!
THE BERMUDA TRIANGLE IS A VERY WELL-TRAVELED AREA AND NOT EVERY SHIP OR PLANE THAT PASSES THROUGH DISAPPEARS!!
STRANGE THINGS ARE GOING ON THERE!
FINISH YOUR SPINACH!
EAT AT MOM'S
ATLANTIC OCEAN
THE AREA COVERS ABOUT 44,000 SQUARE MILES!
THEY'RE ALL GONE!
THE BERMUDA TRIANGLE RUNS FROM THE BERMUDA ISLANDS, SOUTH TO PUERTO RICO, AND WEST TO MIAMI, FLORIDA.
GULF OF MEXICO
FLORIDA
WHAT HAPPENED TO THEM?
NOBODY KNOWS!
THIS IS THE MARTIN MARINER "FLYING BOAT"-WE WERE SENT TO SEARCH FOR FLIGHT 19.
WE'RE EXPERIENCIN HIGH WINDS... ...CLICK!!
FORT LAUDERDALE
I'M LOST!
MIAMI
FIVE OF THE PLANES OF FLIGHT 19 WERE ON A TRAINING MISSION.
COMMUNICATIONS WITH THE MARINER STOPPED SUDDENLY
ON DECEMBER 5, 1945, SIX U.S. NAVY PLANES AND THEIR CREWS DISAPPEARED FOREVER.
FLIGHT 19 ORIGINATED IN FORT LAUDERDALE, FLORIDA.
THE COMMANDER OF FLIGHT 19 WAS LIEUTENANT CHARLES TAYLOR.
ALL 14 MEMBERS OF THE CREW WERE EXPERIENCED FLYERS.
I'VE FLOWN OVER THAT AREA.
LIEUTENANT TAYLOR SENT A STRANGE MESSAGE TO THE NAVAL AIR TOWER AT FORT LAUDERDALE.
CUBA
THEY WERE PRACTICING BOMBING RUNS.
HE SAID IT WA AN EMERGEN THEY SEEME BE OFF COUR THEY COULD SEE LAND.
I SMELL GOOD.
CARIBBEAN SEA
THE MYSTERIOUS DISAPPEARANCE OF FLIGHT 19 HAS BEEN CALLED THE "MARY CELESTE" OF THE SKY.
THIS INCIDENT, THE DISAPPEARANCE OF FLIGHT 19 GAVE THE BERMUDA TRIANGLE ITS NAME.
MORE STRAN MESSAGES FOLLOWED: COMPASSES OUT... WE THI WE'RE OVER FLORIDA KEY
I'M DOING THE WAVE.
I'M GLAD I WASN'T SHIP-WRECKED THERE.
JAMAICA
STATIC MAD THEIR MESSA HARD TO HE THEIR RADIO SIGNAL FAD OUT!
LET'S STAY HERE.

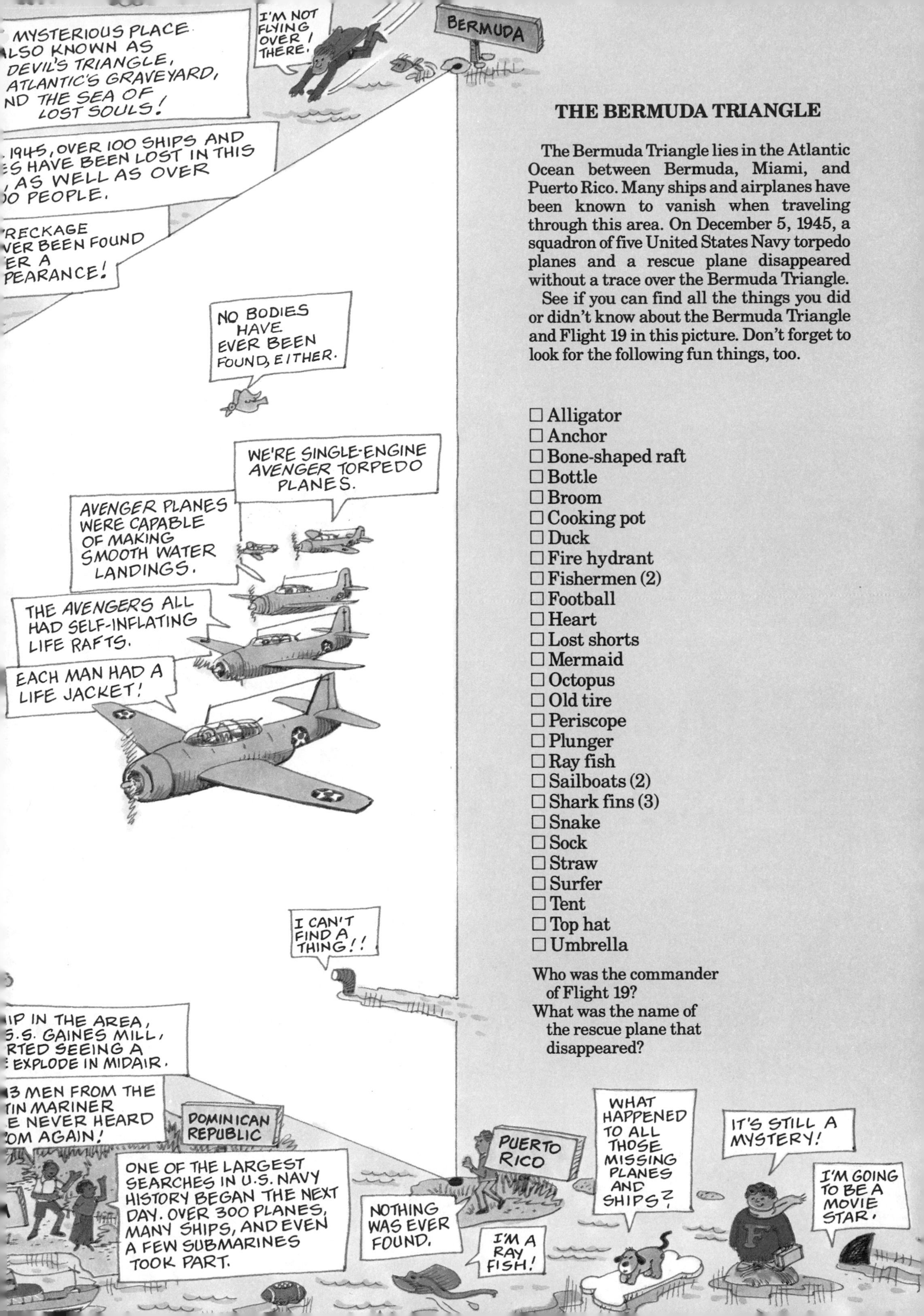

THE BERMUDA TRIANGLE

The Bermuda Triangle lies in the Atlantic Ocean between Bermuda, Miami, and Puerto Rico. Many ships and airplanes have been known to vanish when traveling through this area. On December 5, 1945, a squadron of five United States Navy torpedo planes and a rescue plane disappeared without a trace over the Bermuda Triangle.

See if you can find all the things you did or didn't know about the Bermuda Triangle and Flight 19 in this picture. Don't forget to look for the following fun things, too.

- ☐ Alligator
- ☐ Anchor
- ☐ Bone-shaped raft
- ☐ Bottle
- ☐ Broom
- ☐ Cooking pot
- ☐ Duck
- ☐ Fire hydrant
- ☐ Fishermen (2)
- ☐ Football
- ☐ Heart
- ☐ Lost shorts
- ☐ Mermaid
- ☐ Octopus
- ☐ Old tire
- ☐ Periscope
- ☐ Plunger
- ☐ Ray fish
- ☐ Sailboats (2)
- ☐ Shark fins (3)
- ☐ Snake
- ☐ Sock
- ☐ Straw
- ☐ Surfer
- ☐ Tent
- ☐ Top hat
- ☐ Umbrella

Who was the commander of Flight 19?

What was the name of the rescue plane that disappeared?

LOCH NESS MONSTER

In 1933, a Scottish couple was driving along the new modern road on the northern shore of the Loch Ness lake. Suddenly, their attention was drawn to the center of the lake. They claimed they saw an enormous animal "rolling and plunging" in the water. Since that day there have been over 3,000 reported sightings of the Loch Ness monster.

See if you can find all the things you did or didn't know about the Loch Ness monster in this picture. Don't forget to look for the following fun things, too.

- ☐ Astronaut
- ☐ Balloons (4)
- ☐ Bone
- ☐ Bucket
- ☐ Cameras (2)
- ☐ Clown
- ☐ Duck
- ☐ Fishbowl
- ☐ Flower
- ☐ Ghost
- ☐ Giraffe
- ☐ Golfer
- ☐ Graduate
- ☐ Lost boot
- ☐ Mailbox
- ☐ Mouse
- ☐ Mummy
- ☐ Net
- ☐ Note-in-a-bottle
- ☐ Periscope
- ☐ Pig
- ☐ Sailboat
- ☐ Santa
- ☐ Shorts
- ☐ Skateboard
- ☐ Star
- ☐ Sword
- ☐ Telescope
- ☐ Top hat
- ☐ Turtle

What is the monster's nickname?

How deep is Loch Nes

I'M NOT COMING OUT!
I THINK I SEE SOMETHING!
NESSIE TOURS
NO DEFINITE PROOF HAS YET BEEN FOUND TO PROVE THAT A MONSTER EXISTS IN THE LOCH!
OTHER LARGE LAKES IN SCOTLAND AND IRELAND ARE SUPPOSED TO HAVE MONSTERS IN THEM, TOO.
SOME SCIENTISTS THINK NESSIE IS A HUGE UNKNOWN KIND OF SEA SLUG!
IT'S SUPPOSED TO BE REDDISH-BROWN IN COLOR.
REAL NESSIE TAFFY
NESSIE PIZZA
NESSIE BURGERS
NESSIE COOKIES
ESSIE CONDOS
BE BUILT HERE!
NESSIE ICE CREAM
NESSIE JELLY BEANS
NESSIE NUTS
I'M NOT GOING IN THAT WATER.
I, DETECTIVE DONALD, DETECT TROUBLE.
SWIM AT YOUR OWN RISK
IN 1969, SONAR DETECTED A VERY LARGE OBJECT ABOUT 500 FEET BELOW THE SURFACE.
SONAR SENDS OUT PULSES OF SOUND AND MEASURES ANY ECHOES THAT BOUNCE BACK.
?
I THINK I SEE IT!
I NEVER SAW IT!
I WONDER IF ANYTHING INTERESTING IS GOING ON UP THERE?
DO NOT FEED NESSIE
WOW!
THOUSANDS OF TOURISTS COME HERE EACH YEAR HOPING TO SEE NESSIE.
GET YOUR POSTCARDS HERE!
I DON'T WANT TO BE SEEN HERE!
NESSIE SOUNDS LIKE A BIG FISH STORY TO ME.
NESSIE CAN'T DO THIS!
IS THIS THE MOON?
IN 1972, M.I.T. (MASSACHUSETTES INSTITUTE OF TECHNOLOGY) USED SONAR AND A CAMERA TO TAKE THREE PHOTOS THAT SEEMED TO SHOW A LARGE ANIMAL.
UNFORTUNATELY, THE MURKY WATER BLURRED THE PHOTOS.
MOST DESCRIPTIONS AGREE THAT NESSIE HAS A LARGE BODY...
...A LONG NECK AND SMALL HEAD...
...HAS FOUR POWERFUL FLIPPERS...
...IS BETWEEN 20-30 FEET LONG.
IT'S STILL A MYSTERY!
DOES THE LOCH NESS MONSTER REALLY EXIST?

THIS MUST BE THE PLACE.

STONEHENGE

Stonehenge is an ancient monument built on Salisbury Plain in Wiltshire, England. For centuries, scientists have puzzled over the circular arrangement of this group of huge, rough-cut stones and holes in the ground. Archeologists believe Stonehenge was shaped and positioned by a group of people over 3,300 years ago without the aid of modern tools and equipment. No ne knows exactly how this was accomplished.

See if you can find all the things you did or didn't know about Stonehenge in this picture. Don't forget to look for the following fun things, too.

- ☐ Arrow
- ☐ Bird
- ☐ Bone
- ☐ Book
- ☐ Clown face
- ☐ Cooking pot
- ☐ Crown
- ☐ Cupcake
- ☐ Duck
- ☐ Elephant
- ☐ Flower
- ☐ Flying saucer
- ☐ Football
- ☐ Guitar
- ☐ Handbag
- ☐ Horse
- ☐ Jogger
- ☐ Magic wand
- ☐ Merlin
- ☐ Palm tree
- ☐ Pencil
- ☐ Pick
- ☐ Pig
- ☐ Rabbit
- ☐ Shovel
- ☐ Teapot
- ☐ Tennis racket
- ☐ Turtle
- ☐ Umbrella
- ☐ Worm

How many stones were used to build Stonehenge?

How much do the heaviest stones weigh?

AMELIA EARHART

In the early 1900's, flight was a new and sometimes frightening wonder. In 1908, when Amelia Earhart first saw an airplane soar among the clouds, she was fascinated. Amelia Earhart became a pioneer in the new world of aviation and in 1932 she made history as the first woman to fly solo across the Atlantic Ocean.

See if you can find all the things you did or didn't know about Amelia Earhart in this picture. Don't forget to look for the following fun things, too.

- ☐ Apple
- ☐ Basketball hoop
- ☐ Bell
- ☐ Chef's hat
- ☐ Envelope
- ☐ File folder
- ☐ Fish (2)
- ☐ Fishbowl
- ☐ Football
- ☐ Fork
- ☐ Graduate
- ☐ Hamburger
- ☐ Hammer
- ☐ Jack-o'-lantern
- ☐ Key
- ☐ Lost sock
- ☐ Magnifying glass
- ☐ Mouse
- ☐ Nurse
- ☐ Old radio
- ☐ Old telephone
- ☐ Paper airplane
- ☐ Pencil
- ☐ Pizza
- ☐ School spirit
- ☐ Seal
- ☐ Target
- ☐ Tennis racket
- ☐ Toaster
- ☐ TV set
- ☐ Typewriter
- ☐ Wastepaper basket
- ☐ Yo-yo

What was Amelia's great ambition as a pilot?

THE SHE DED ABIA RSITY.
HER REAL LOVE WAS FLYING. SHE DROPPED OUT TO EARN MONEY FOR FLYING LESSONS.
SHE LEARNED TO FLY IN LOS ANGELES, CALIFORNIA AND IN 1928 BECAME THE FIRST WOMAN TO FLY ACROSS THE ATLANTIC OCEAN.
SHE FLEW WITH WILBUR STUNTZ AND LOUIS GORDON.
THE PLANE WAS NAMED "FRIENDSHIP!"
SHE WROTE A BOOK ABOUT HER FLIGHT AND LATER MARRIED HER PUBLISHER, GEORGE PUTNAM.
LEW IN A ENGINE EED 10-E CTRA ANE.
THE PLANE VANISHED SOMEWHERE BETWEEN NEW GUINEA AND HOWLAND ISLAND.
SOME THINK THAT THEY WERE SHOT DOWN BY THE JAPANESE WHO BELIEVED THEY WERE ON A SECRET SPY MISSION.
OTHERS BELIEVE THEY WERE TESTING AN EXPERIMENTAL PLANE ON A SPECIAL GOVERNMENT MISSION AND WERE SECRETLY FLOWN BACK TO THE U.S. AND GIVEN NEW IDENTITIES.
THESE ARE GREAT COMIC STRIPS FOR OUR SCHOOL PAPER.
FREDDIE, LISA, AND LAURA ARE IN IT.
AMELIA EARHART'S FIRST ATTEMPT AT A ROUND-THE-WORLD FLIGHT ALMOST ENDED IN TRAGEDY. A TIRE BLOW-OUT WHILE TAXIING RESULTED IN CONSIDERABLE DAMAGE TO THE PLANE....
WHEN HER LOCKHEED ELECTRA WAS REPAIRED, MISS EARHART CHANGED HER DIRECTION. WITH NAVIGATOR FRED NOONAN, SHE TOOK OFF IN HER "FLYING LABORATORY," HEADING EASTWARD OUT OF MIAMI, ON THE GRAY MORNING OF JUNE 1, 1937.

WHEN AMELIA EARHART TOOK OFF ON HER ROUND-THE-WORLD LIGHT, HER PLANE WAS WELL-EQUIP-ED WITH RUBBER RAFTS, FLARES, AND THER SAFETY DEVICES. ENOUGH URVIVAL EQUIPMENT TO MEET ALMOST ANY EVENTUALITY....
F

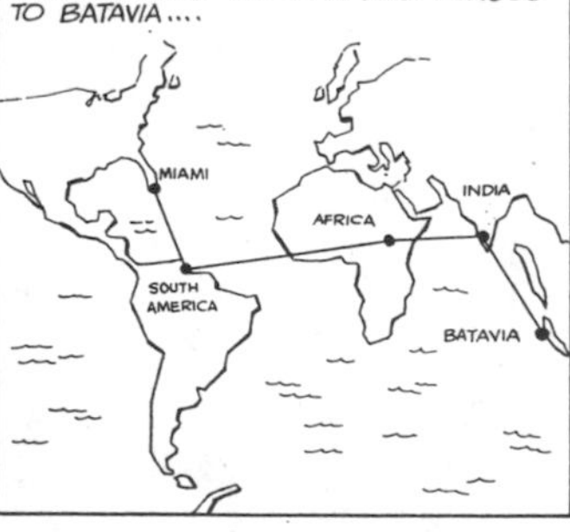

MISS EARHART FLEW A SOUTH EASTERLY ROUTE FROM MIAMI TO SOUTH AMERICA; THEN ON TO AFRICA. FROM THERE, SHE EASILY HOPPED TO INDIA AND ACROSS TO BATAVIA....
MIAMI
AFRICA
INDIA
SOUTH AMERICA
BATAVIA

HOWLAND ISLAND WAS TO BE THE LAST STOP BEFORE HONOLULU. A TINY, 2-MILE-SQUARE SPECK IN THE OCEAN.... A DIFFICULT TARGET FOR ANY PILOT....

AT 7:42 A.M., ON JULY 2, 1937, THE U.S. CUTTER ITASCA, WAITING AT HOWLAND ISLAND, RECEIVED THIS RADIO MESSAGE: "WE MUST BE ON YOU, BUT WE CANNOT SEE YOU. GAS IS RUNNING LOW. BEEN UNABLE TO REACH YOU BY RADIO...."

DURING THE NEXT DAYS, ONE OF THE LARGEST SEARCHES IN HISTORY TOOK PLACE. MEN, SHIPS, AND PLANES OF THREE NATIONS, INCLUDING JAPANESE AIRCRAFT, ENGAGED IN THE TREMENDOUS, EXHAUSTIVE HUNT....
2-J-14

THE OPERATION COST $1,000,000! THAT WAS 55 YEARS AGO. NOT ONE AUTHENTICATED CLUE TO THE FATE OF MISS EARHART, NAVIGATOR NOONAN, OR THEIR PLANE HAS EVER BEEN FOUND!
107

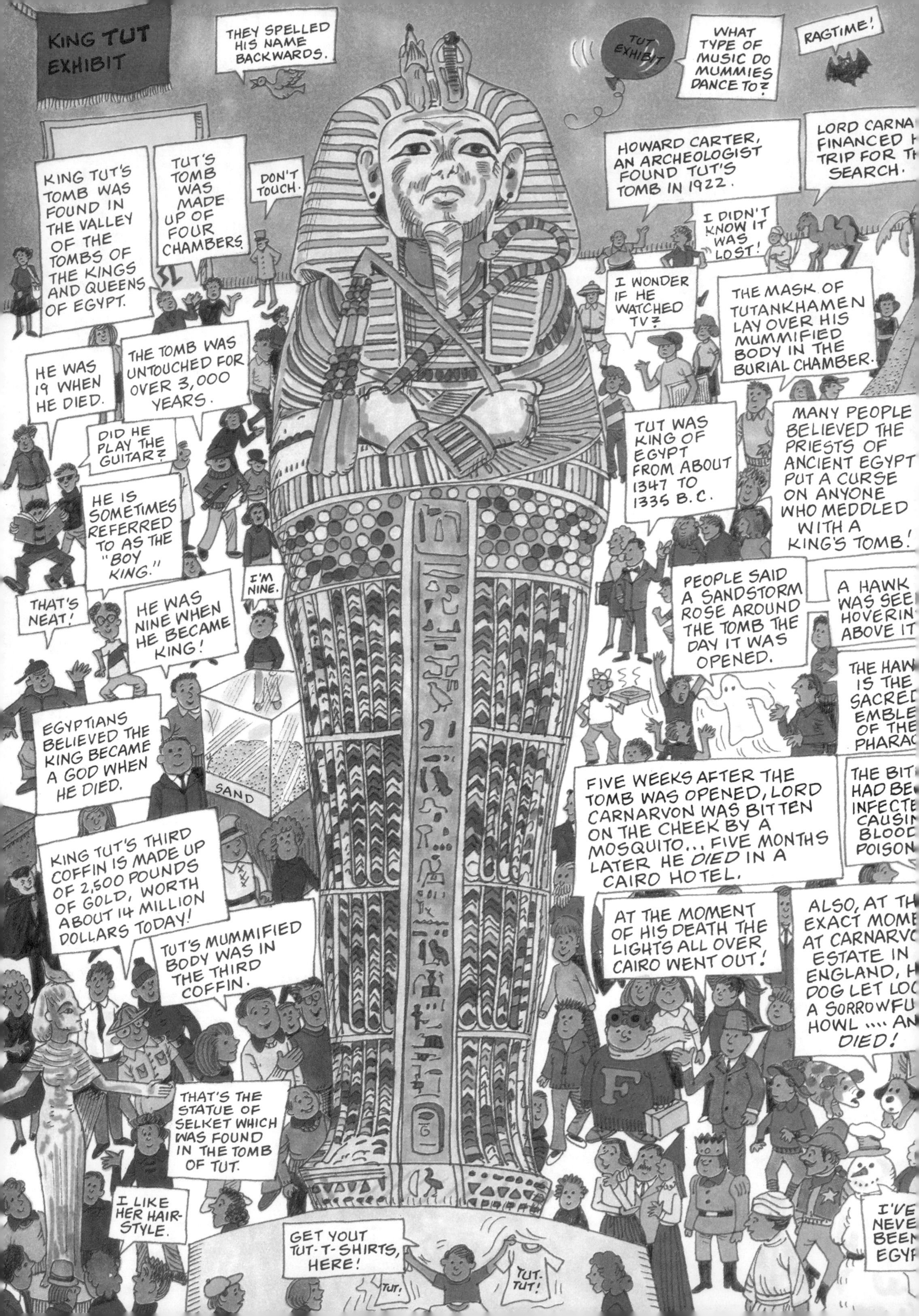

KING TUT EXHIBIT
THEY SPELLED HIS NAME BACKWARDS.
TUT EXHIBIT
WHAT TYPE OF MUSIC DO MUMMIES DANCE TO?
RAGTIME!
KING TUT'S TOMB WAS FOUND IN THE VALLEY OF THE TOMBS OF THE KINGS AND QUEENS OF EGYPT.
TUT'S TOMB WAS MADE UP OF FOUR CHAMBERS.
DON'T TOUCH.
HOWARD CARTER, AN ARCHEOLOGIST FOUND TUT'S TOMB IN 1922.
LORD CARNA FINANCED H TRIP FOR TH SEARCH.
I DIDN'T KNOW IT WAS LOST!
I WONDER IF HE WATCHED TV?
THE MASK OF TUTANKHAMEN LAY OVER HIS MUMMIFIED BODY IN THE BURIAL CHAMBER.
HE WAS 19 WHEN HE DIED.
THE TOMB WAS UNTOUCHED FOR OVER 3,000 YEARS.
DID HE PLAY THE GUITAR?
TUT WAS KING OF EGYPT FROM ABOUT 1347 TO 1335 B.C.
MANY PEOPLE BELIEVED THE PRIESTS OF ANCIENT EGYPT PUT A CURSE ON ANYONE WHO MEDDLED WITH A KING'S TOMB!
HE IS SOMETIMES REFERRED TO AS THE "BOY KING."
THAT'S NEAT!
I'M NINE.
HE WAS NINE WHEN HE BECAME KING!
PEOPLE SAID A SANDSTORM ROSE AROUND THE TOMB THE DAY IT WAS OPENED.
A HAWK WAS SEE HOVERIN ABOVE IT
THE HAW IS THE SACRED EMBLE OF THE PHARA
EGYPTIANS BELIEVED THE KING BECAME A GOD WHEN HE DIED.
SAND
FIVE WEEKS AFTER THE TOMB WAS OPENED, LORD CARNARVON WAS BITTEN ON THE CHEEK BY A MOSQUITO... FIVE MONTHS LATER HE *DIED* IN A CAIRO HOTEL.
THE BIT HAD BE INFECTE CAUSIN BLOOD POISON
KING TUT'S THIRD COFFIN IS MADE UP OF 2,500 POUNDS OF GOLD, WORTH ABOUT 14 MILLION DOLLARS TODAY!
TUT'S MUMMIFIED BODY WAS IN THE THIRD COFFIN.
AT THE MOMENT OF HIS DEATH THE LIGHTS ALL OVER CAIRO WENT OUT!
ALSO, AT TH EXACT MOME AT CARNARVO ESTATE IN ENGLAND, H DOG LET LOO A SORROWFU HOWL .... AN *DIED!*
F
THAT'S THE STATUE OF SELKET WHICH WAS FOUND IN THE TOMB OF TUT.
I LIKE HER HAIR-STYLE.
GET YOUT TUT-T-SHIRTS, HERE!
TUT!
TUT. TUT!
I'VE NEVE BEEN EGYP

KING TUT'S CURSE

Howard Carter's 30 year search was over. On November 26, 1922, he stood before the entrance to the lost tomb of the "boy king," Tutankhamen. Entering, he stared in disbelief at the gold, jewels, and other treasures before him. However, that day, a hawk, sacred symbol of the Pharaohs, was seen soaring above the tomb. Many say this signalled the beginning of the Pharaoh's curse.

See if you can find all the things you did or didn't know about King Tut's curse in this picture. Don't forget to look for the following fun things, too.

- ☐ Balloon
- ☐ Banana peel
- ☐ Broom
- ☐ Camel
- ☐ Crown
- ☐ Fire hydrant
- ☐ Fish
- ☐ Flying bat
- ☐ Football player
- ☐ Ghost
- ☐ Horn
- ☐ Horseshoe
- ☐ Kite
- ☐ Lost medal
- ☐ Mouse
- ☐ Mummy and child
- ☐ Pencil
- ☐ Pizza delivery
- ☐ Sailor
- ☐ Sand
- ☐ Shovel
- ☐ Skier
- ☐ Snake
- ☐ Snowman
- ☐ Star
- ☐ Stethoscope
- ☐ Tin man
- ☐ Top hat
- ☐ Vase

What happened to Lord Carnarvon?
What was unusual about the scar on Tut's cheek?

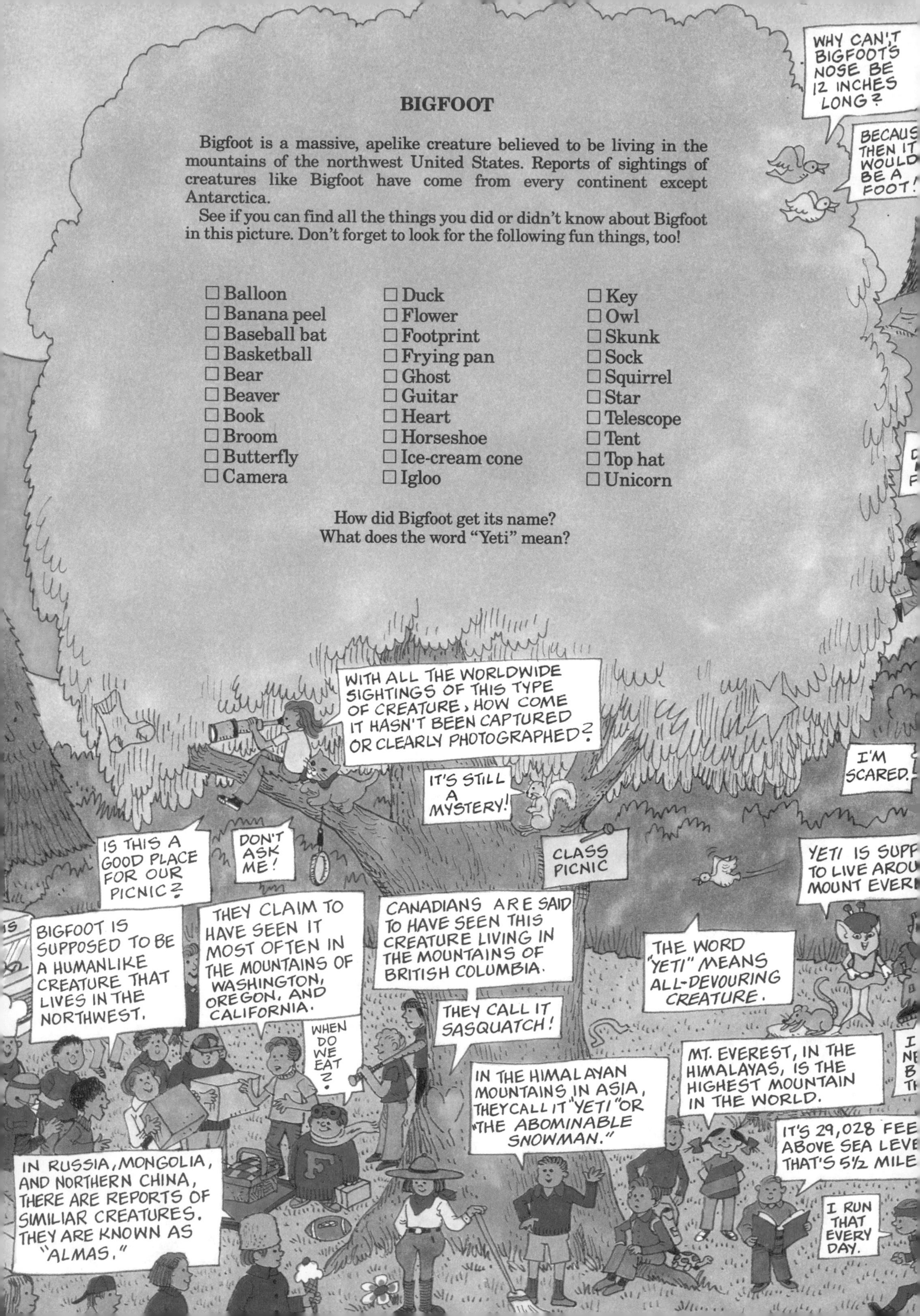

BIGFOOT

Bigfoot is a massive, apelike creature believed to be living in the mountains of the northwest United States. Reports of sightings of creatures like Bigfoot have come from every continent except Antarctica.

See if you can find all the things you did or didn't know about Bigfoot in this picture. Don't forget to look for the following fun things, too!

- ☐ Balloon
- ☐ Banana peel
- ☐ Baseball bat
- ☐ Basketball
- ☐ Bear
- ☐ Beaver
- ☐ Book
- ☐ Broom
- ☐ Butterfly
- ☐ Camera
- ☐ Duck
- ☐ Flower
- ☐ Footprint
- ☐ Frying pan
- ☐ Ghost
- ☐ Guitar
- ☐ Heart
- ☐ Horseshoe
- ☐ Ice-cream cone
- ☐ Igloo
- ☐ Key
- ☐ Owl
- ☐ Skunk
- ☐ Sock
- ☐ Squirrel
- ☐ Star
- ☐ Telescope
- ☐ Tent
- ☐ Top hat
- ☐ Unicorn

How did Bigfoot get its name?
What does the word "Yeti" mean?

IF BIGFOOT HAD 3 FEET HE'D BE CALLED BIGYARD!
IT CAN'T BE REAL!
DID SOMEBODY CALL ME?
CALL THE ZOO!
CALL THE U.N.!
CALL THE TV STATION!
QUACK! BETTER DUCK.
I'M CALLING FOR HELP!
DEER, THAT'S ME.
ARE MY EYES PLAYING TRICKS ON ME?
BIGFOOT LIKES TO HAVE FRANK-FOOTERS FOR LUNCH.
I THINK I SEE IT!
GULP!
NO ONE WANTS TO BE UNDERFOOT WHEN HE'S AROUND!
S SAID TO BE A CREATURE WITH GE APELIKE AND A HUMAN-E FACE.
THE STORIES ABOUT THE ABOMINABLE SNOWMAN SAY THAT IT COMES DOWN FROM THE MOUNTAINS TO ATTACK VILLAGERS!!
FOOT IS OSED TO -10 FEET ND WEIGH R 500 NDS.
ITS FOOTPRINTS MEASURE 17 INCHES LONG AND 6 INCHES WIDE. THIS IS HOW IT GOT ITS NAME-BIGFOOT!
DOES IT PLAY PRO-BASKETBALL?
MAYBE SO... MAYBE NO!
WHERE DOES IT BUY ITS SHOES?
REALLY?
NEAR BOSSBURG, WASHINGTON, A SERIES OF 1,089 PERFECT FOOTPRINTS WERE FOUND.
THAT'S A BIG FOOT.
AM I INVITED?

HI, MOM!
PLATO WAS THE FIRST TO DESCRIBE ATLANTIS.
ACCORDING TO PLATO, ATLANTIS WAS AN ISLAND IN THE ATLANTIC OCEAN PAST THE STRAITS OF GILBRALTAR. THE STRAITS WERE KNOWN THEN AS "THE PILLARS OF HERCULES."
CONDOS FOR SALE
THIS GREAT EMPIRE WAS RULED BY TEN KINGS FROM A CIRCULAR WALLED CITY AT THE CENTER.
THIS IS HEAVY.
PLATO WAS A GREEK PHILOSOPHER WHO LIVED OVER 2400 YEARS AGO.
THE ATLANTEANS WERE A RICH AND POWERFUL PEOPLE WHO CONQUERED MOST OF THE KNOWN WORLD.
ARE WE GOING TO HAVE ANOTHER EARTHQUAKE?
THE ISLAND TEEMED WITH WILDLIFE.
THEY WERE FINALLY DEFEATED BY ATHENS.
PLATO BASED HIS STORY OF ATLANTIS ON SOLON'S DESCRIPTION OF ATLANTIS WRITTEN 200 YEARS BEFORE.
SOLON GOT HIS INFORMATION FROM EGYPTIAN WRITINGS.
ACCORDING TO LEGEND, ATLANTIS WAS FIRST RULED BY POSEIDON, THE GOD OF THE SEA.
AFTERWARDS, EARTHQUAKES ROCKED AND TOPPLED ATLANTIS AND FLOODS FROM THE RESULTING TIDAL WAVE SUBMERGED IT!
MAKE MY DAY!
THE TEN KINGS, WERE POSEIDON'S SONS.
HEAVY RAINS SANK IT UNDER THE SEA.
I'M AN UNCLE AND AN ANT.
DON'T ASK ME ... I'M LOST!
WHERE AM I?
BAA!
WHAT'S THE RUSH?
THIS IS ATLANTIS?
I'M GOING BACK.
GET OFF ME!

ATLANTIS

The idea of a perfect world—one filled with beauty, peace, and happiness—had kept man searching for the lost island of Atlantis for centuries. Was Atlantis a real place, or just an ancient Egyptian myth made popular by Plato?

See if you can find all the things you did or didn't know about Atlantis in this picture. Don't forget to look for the following fun things, too.

☐ Ant	☐ Flamingo	☐ Owl	☐ Snake
☐ Axe	☐ Frog	☐ Ox	☐ Sock
☐ Book	☐ Guitar	☐ Paintbrush	☐ Toucan
☐ Chef's hat	☐ Heart	☐ Pelican	☐ Turtle
☐ Chicken	☐ Ice-cream cone	☐ Periscope	☐ Umbrella
☐ Deep-sea diver	☐ Kite	☐ Pig	☐ Unicorn
☐ Deer	☐ Lion	☐ Rhinoceros	☐ Zebra
☐ Elephant	☐ Mermaid	☐ Snail	

Who was Plato?

Some scientists believe Atlantis was what island?

SOME PEOPLE THOUGHT AMERICA WAS ATLANTIS AND THAT THE MAYANS, INCAS, AND AZTECS WERE THEIR HIGHLY CIVILIZED ANCESTORS.
SOME PEOPLE THINK THE ATLANTEANS WERE SPACEMEN WHO BUILT STONEHENGE, EGYPT'S PYRAMIDS, AND THE GIANT HEADS ON EASTER ISLAND.
I'M STAYING RIGHT HERE.
Z-Z-Z-Z!
OVER 2,000 BOOKS HAVE BEEN WRITTEN ABOUT ATLANTIS!
I READ THEM ALL.
I SAW THE MOVIE.
I WATCHED THE TV SERIES.
TLY, SCIENTISTS
E THEY HAVE
ATLANTIS.
THEY THINK IT'S ACTUALLY THE ISLAND OF THERA.
TODAY, THERA IS KNOWN AS SANTORIN IN THE AEGEAN SEA.
I'LL OPEN A RESTAURANT HERE.
ITS HISTORY MATCHES THE STORY OF ATLANTIS CLOSELY.
THE MINOAN PEOPLE LIVED ON THERA AND ON THE NEARBY ISLAND OF CRETE.
GREECE
AEGEAN SEA
TURKE
I'M SEASICK!
THE MINOAN S WERE RICH AND POWERFUL. THEY HAD A VERY ADVANCED CULTURE.
MEDITERRANEAN SEA
THERA
CRETE
ATLANTIS WAS SUPPOSED TO BE THE PERFECT SOCIETY!
DID THEY HAVE HOME-WORK?
A VOLCANO ERUPTED ON THERA AROUND 1500 B.C. THIS IS ABOUT THE SAME TIME ATLANTIS DISAPPEARED.
THE VOLCANIC ERUPTION AND TIDAL WAVE DESTROYED MOST OF THERA AND CRETE!
F ATLANTIS DID
EXIST, WHERE
WAS IT?
IT'S STILL A MYSTERY!
I'VE NEVER BEEN THERE!

ANOTHER JONAH

Like the biblical Jonah, James Bartley was swallowed by a whale. In 1891, Bartley, a young British seaman, was making his first voyage aboard the whaler, *Star of the East.* While in pursuit of a whale, Bartley was thrown overboard and thought to have drowned.

See if you can find all the things you did or didn't know about James Bartley, another Jonah, in this picture. Don't forget to look for the following fun things, too.

- ☐ Anchor
- ☐ Barrel
- ☐ Basket
- ☐ Birdcage
- ☐ Blackboard
- ☐ Bow tie
- ☐ Bugle
- ☐ Can
- ☐ Coffeepot
- ☐ Crab
- ☐ Cup
- ☐ Fish hook
- ☐ Flowerpot
- ☐ Football
- ☐ Ghost
- ☐ Hammer
- ☐ Hockey stick
- ☐ Horseshoe
- ☐ Necklace
- ☐ Oar
- ☐ Pencil
- ☐ Pocket watch
- ☐ Sailboat
- ☐ Scissors
- ☐ Seahorse
- ☐ Shark
- ☐ Shirt
- ☐ Snail
- ☐ Sneaker
- ☐ Starfish
- ☐ Swordfish
- ☐ Thermometer
- ☐ Tire
- ☐ Yo-yo

What kind of whale was the *Star of the East* hunting?
How old was James Bartley when this happened?

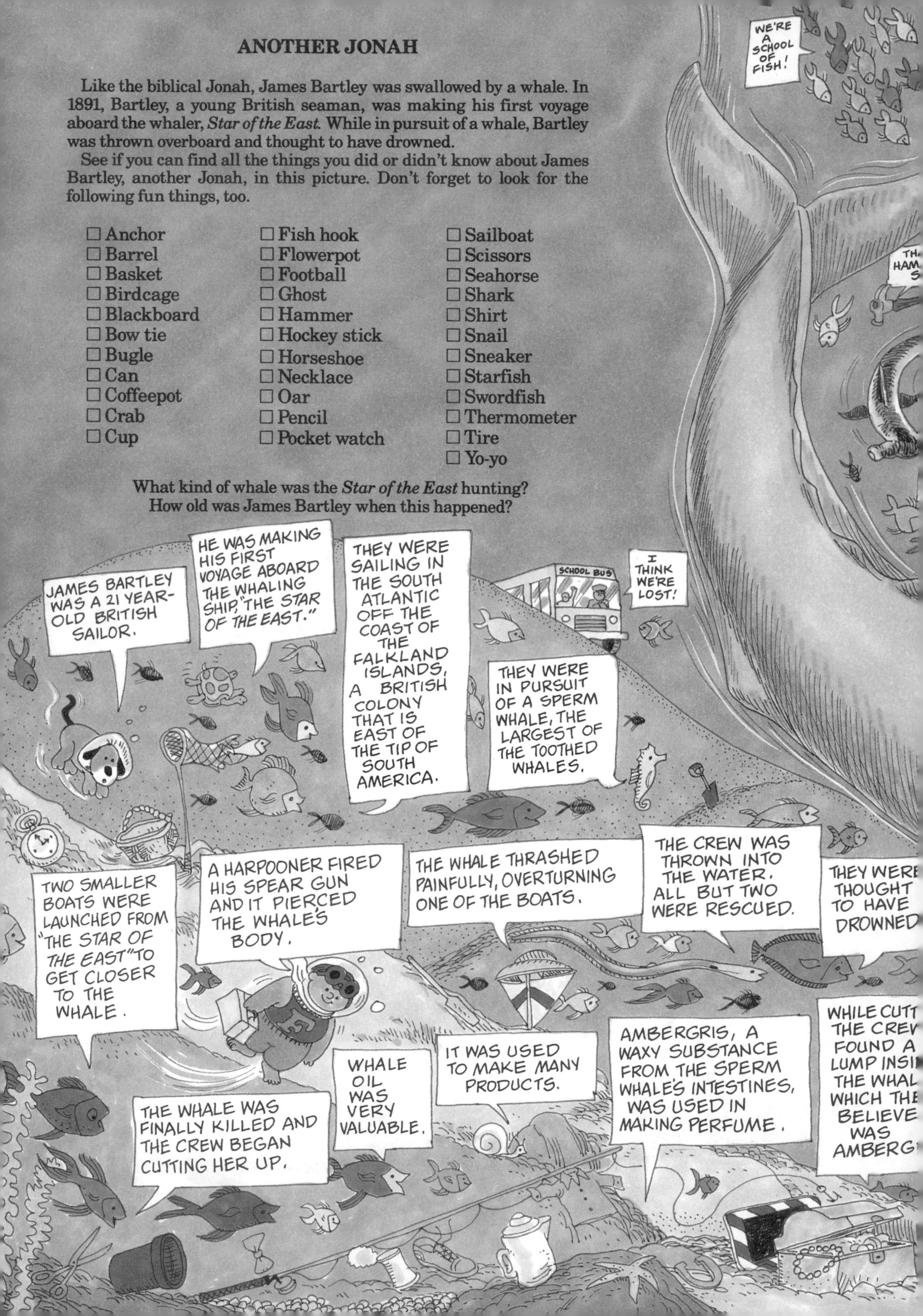

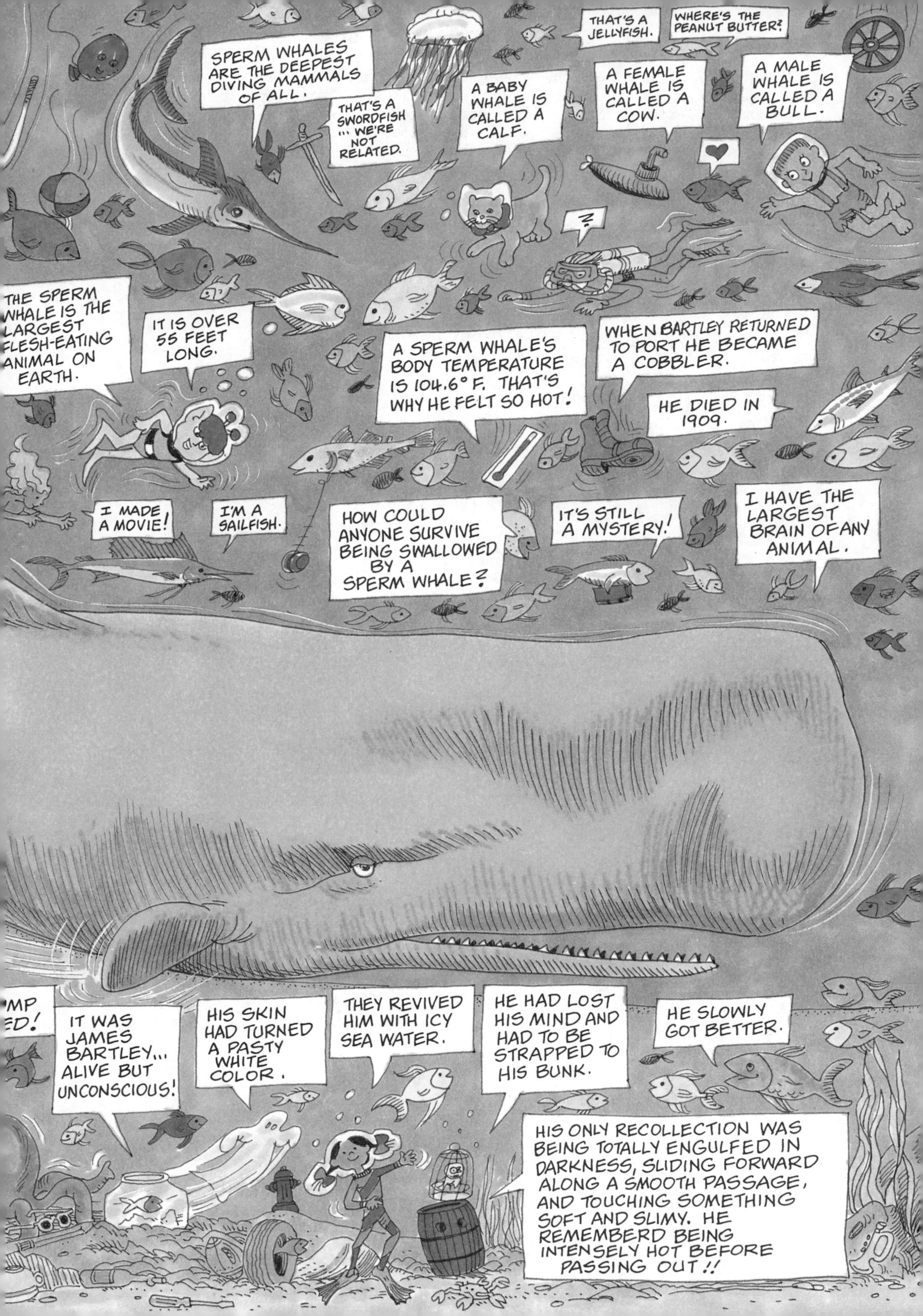
SPERM WHALES ARE THE DEEPEST DIVING MAMMALS OF ALL.
THAT'S A SWORDFISH ... WE'RE NOT RELATED.
THAT'S A JELLYFISH.
WHERE'S THE PEANUT BUTTER?
A BABY WHALE IS CALLED A CALF.
A FEMALE WHALE IS CALLED A COW.
A MALE WHALE IS CALLED A BULL.
THE SPERM WHALE IS THE LARGEST FLESH-EATING ANIMAL ON EARTH.
IT IS OVER 55 FEET LONG.
A SPERM WHALE'S BODY TEMPERATURE IS 104.6° F. THAT'S WHY HE FELT SO HOT!
WHEN BARTLEY RETURNED TO PORT HE BECAME A COBBLER.
HE DIED IN 1909.
I MADE A MOVIE!
I'M A SAILFISH.
HOW COULD ANYONE SURVIVE BEING SWALLOWED BY A SPERM WHALE?
IT'S STILL A MYSTERY!
I HAVE THE LARGEST BRAIN OF ANY ANIMAL.
IT WAS JAMES BARTLEY... ALIVE BUT UNCONSCIOUS!
HIS SKIN HAD TURNED A PASTY WHITE COLOR.
THEY REVIVED HIM WITH ICY SEA WATER.
HE HAD LOST HIS MIND AND HAD TO BE STRAPPED TO HIS BUNK.
HE SLOWLY GOT BETTER.
HIS ONLY RECOLLECTION WAS BEING TOTALLY ENGULFED IN DARKNESS, SLIDING FORWARD ALONG A SMOOTH PASSAGE, AND TOUCHING SOMETHING SOFT AND SLIMY. HE REMEMBERD BEING INTENSELY HOT BEFORE PASSING OUT!!

THE TUNGUSKA EXPLOSION

On June 30, 1908, the sky over the icy wilderness of Siberia flashed with a bright streak of light. Suddenly, the earth shook and smoke and fire shot up into the sky reaching a height of 10 miles. This tremendous explosion was recorded around the world.

See if you can find all the things you did or didn't know about the Tunguska Explosion in this picture. Don't forget to look for the following fun things, too.

- ☐ Arrow
- ☐ Bat
- ☐ Bear
- ☐ Bell
- ☐ Birdbath
- ☐ Boot
- ☐ Camel
- ☐ Crayon
- ☐ Crown
- ☐ Cupcake
- ☐ Doll
- ☐ Drum
- ☐ Elephant
- ☐ Envelope
- ☐ Fish
- ☐ Flashlight
- ☐ Football
- ☐ Fork
- ☐ Ghost
- ☐ Heart
- ☐ Hot-air balloon
- ☐ Hot dog
- ☐ Igloo
- ☐ Jack-o'-lantern
- ☐ Key
- ☐ Kite
- ☐ Lips
- ☐ Mailbox
- ☐ Mask
- ☐ Moon face
- ☐ Mouse
- ☐ Pillow
- ☐ Ring
- ☐ Sailboat
- ☐ Skis
- ☐ Snake
- ☐ Tent
- ☐ Tin can
- ☐ Tire
- ☐ Toothbrush
- ☐ Top hat
- ☐ Tree
- ☐ Tulip
- ☐ Turtle
- ☐ TV set
- ☐ Umbrella

When were atomic bombs first produced?
What is a meteorite?

ON JUNE 30, 1908, THE FAMOUS TUNGUSKA METEORITE CRASHED INTO THE EARTH IN SIBERIA.

SIBERIA IS IN ASIA. IT IS A VAST, ICY, WILDERNESS.

PEOPLE FELT THE EARTH SHAKE 50 MILES AWAY!

IT WAS ESTIMATED TO WEIGH A FEW HUNDRED TONS.

THE FIRE IT CAUSED SCORCHED A 20 MILE AREA OF EARTH.

SMOKE AND FIRE SHOT UP INTO THE SKY TO A HEIGHT OF 10 MILES.

ALL OVE WORL SEISMOG FELT AN RECORD THE EXPLOSIC

PEOPLE 466 MILES AWAY SAW THIS METEOR IN FULL DAYLIGHT.

A METEOR IS A BRIGHT STREAK OF LIGHT.

METEORS ARE KNOWN AS SHOOTING STARS OR FALLING STARS BECAUSE THEY LOOK LIKE STARS FALLING FROM THE SKY.

METEORITES ARE CHUNKS OF METAL OR STONE THAT REACH THE SURFACE OF THE EARTH BEFORE BURNING UP.

FRICTION WITH THE AIR CREATES THE BRIGHT STREAK OF LIGHT.

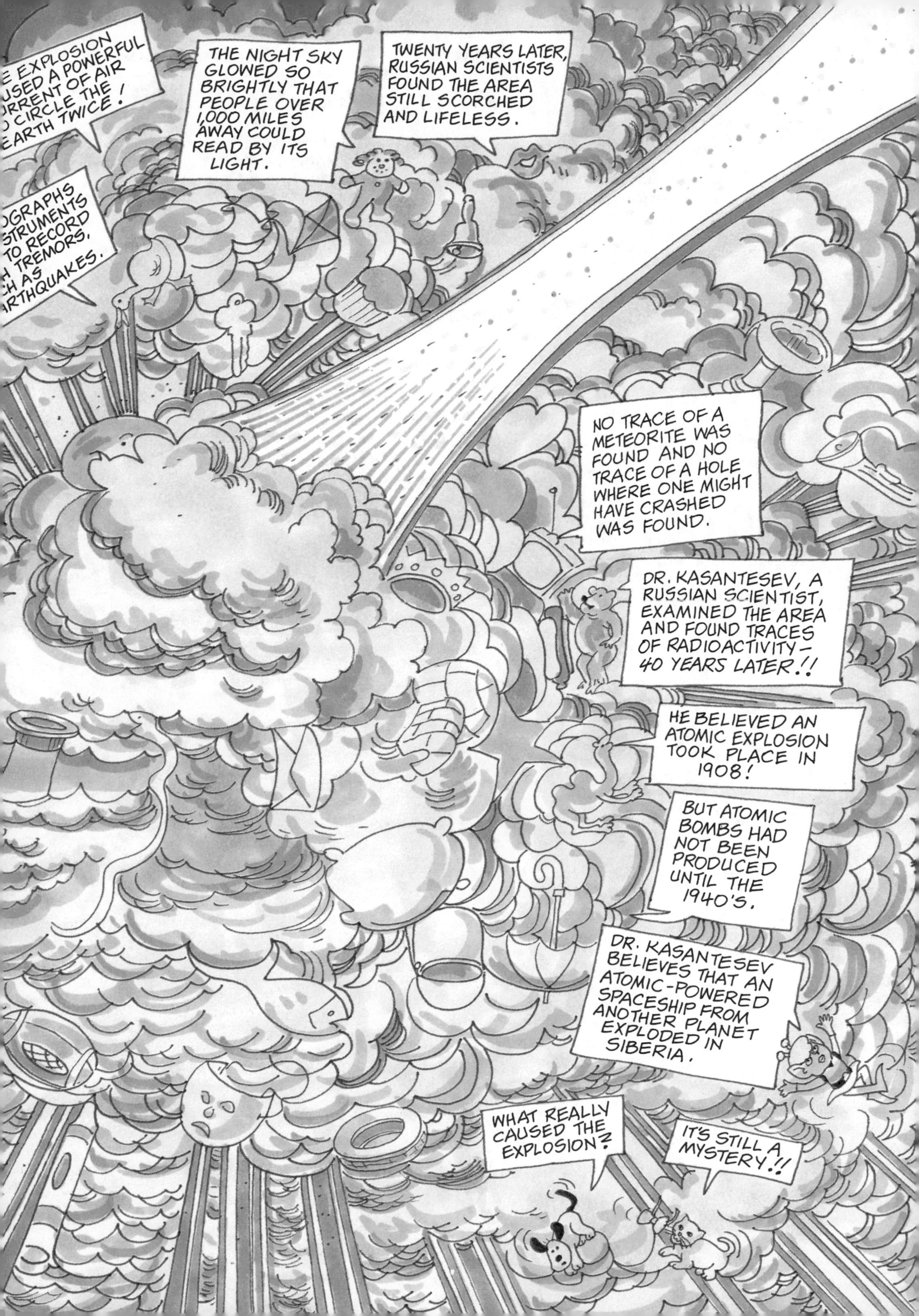
E EXPLOSION USED A POWERFUL URRENT OF AIR O CIRCLE THE EARTH TWICE!
THE NIGHT SKY GLOWED SO BRIGHTLY THAT PEOPLE OVER 1,000 MILES AWAY COULD READ BY ITS LIGHT.
TWENTY YEARS LATER, RUSSIAN SCIENTISTS FOUND THE AREA STILL SCORCHED AND LIFELESS.
OGRAPHS STRUMENTS TO RECORD H TREMORS, CH AS ARTHQUAKES.
NO TRACE OF A METEORITE WAS FOUND AND NO TRACE OF A HOLE WHERE ONE MIGHT HAVE CRASHED WAS FOUND.
DR. KASANTESEV, A RUSSIAN SCIENTIST, EXAMINED THE AREA AND FOUND TRACES OF RADIOACTIVITY– 40 YEARS LATER!!
HE BELIEVED AN ATOMIC EXPLOSION TOOK PLACE IN 1908!
BUT ATOMIC BOMBS HAD NOT BEEN PRODUCED UNTIL THE 1940'S.
DR. KASANTESEV BELIEVES THAT AN ATOMIC-POWERED SPACESHIP FROM ANOTHER PLANET EXPLODED IN SIBERIA.
WHAT REALLY CAUSED THE EXPLOSION?
IT'S STILL A MYSTERY!!

I'LL HELP SOLVE THIS MYSTERY.
I DIDN'T KNOW THAT!
QUACK! ME, TOO!!
I DIDN'T SEE A THING!
THIS IS WHA THEY CALL A BAD LUCK SHIP!
THE MARY CELESTE
The *Mary Celeste* was thought to be "born" unlucky. Built in 1861, this British sailing ship was originally named the *Amazon*. She went through four captains and numerous catastrophes before she was bought by an American and renamed the *Mary Celeste*. Benjamin Briggs, her captain and part owner, set sail from New York to Genoa, Italy in November 1872, but he, his family, and crew vanished in route. The *Mary Celeste* was found in good condition and to this day know one knows what happened.
See if you can find all the things you did or didn't know about the *Mary Celeste* in this picture. Don't forget to look for the following fun things, too!
☐ Balloons (4)
☐ Barrel
☐ Broom
☐ Cactus
☐ Chattering teeth
☐ Chef's hat
☐ Duck
☐ Elephant
☐ Fishing pole
☐ Flamingo
☐ Flowerpot
☐ Flying bats (2)
☐ Ghost
☐ Giraffe
☐ Horseshoe
☐ Hot dog
☐ Humpty Dumpty
☐ Mouse
☐ Octopus
☐ Pelican
☐ Periscope
☐ Saw
☐ Skull and crossbones
☐ Sock
☐ Surfboard
☐ Telescope
☐ Turtle
☐ Umbrella
☐ Whale
☐ Wreath
What cargo was she carrying?
Where was the ship going when this happened?
I'LL PUT SOME LIGHT ON THIS!
THE MARY CELESTE WAS 103 FEET LONG AND WEIGHED 282 TONS.
HER FIRST CAPTAIN DIED SHORTLY AFTER TAKING COMMAND!
ON HER VERY FIRST VOYAGE, SHE DAMAGED HER HULL AND WHILE BEING REPAIRED A FIRE BROKE OUT!
WOW!
?
A MYSTERY SHIP!
WHERE ARE THEY?
THEY'RE ALL LOST.
I SAW THAT.
DURING AN ATLANTIC CROSSING, SHE COLLIDED WITH ANOTHER SHIP. SHE HAD HAD FOUR CAPTAINS BY THEN!
I DIDN'T DO IT!!
MAYBE THE BARRELS OF ALCOHOL GAVE OFF FUMES AND THEY FEARED THE SHIP WOULD EXPLODE!
THIS WATER IS COLD! CHATTER-CHATTER!
ON NOVEMBER 5, 18
CAPTAIN BRIGGS SET SAIL FROM NEW YORK TO GENOA, ITALY.
IN 1867, SHE RAN AGROUND IN NOVA SCOTIA!
DO YOU NEED A HAND?
THEY ABANDONED SHIP AND THE WIND BLEW THE MARY CELESTE AWAY FROM THEM!
THEY WERE LOST AT SEA.
I'VE NEVER BEEN THERE!
HER CARG WAS 170C BARRELS ALCOHOL FUEL.
WAS MERMAID IN A MOVIE?
MAYBE THEY WERE ATTACKED BY ONE OF US.
THE FINAL DAYS OF THE MARY CELESTE CAME IN 1884, WHEN SHE WAS WRECKED ON A CORAL REEF NEAR HAITI FOR INSURANCE MONEY!
THE INSURANCE MONEY WAS NEVER PAID!
I'M GLAD I WORE MY BOOT!

THIS IS MY KIND OF SHIP!
I'M TOO LATE!
THE CREW'S PERSONAL BELONGINGS WERE STILL ON BOARD.
EVERYONE WAS MISSING, BUT NO ONE KNOWS WHY!
THE SHIP WAS IN GOOD CONDITION.
HE CAPTAIN'S STRONGBOX WAS STILL LOCKED N HIS CABIN.
TOO BAD!
?
THE CAPTAIN'S BED WAS UNMADE.
A BOTTLE OF MEDICINE WAS OPEN WITH THE SPOON NEARBY.
HE ONLY NGS MISSING RE SOME SHIP'S PERS, VIGATION OKS, AND UIPMENT!
IT LOOKS LIKE THE CREW HACKED AWAY PART OF THE RAILING TO LAUNCH THE LIFEBOAT.
TIME TO CLEAN UP.
THERE WERE PLENTY OF SUPPLIES IN THE GALLEY.
MARY CELESTE
THE CARGO WAS STILL IN PLACE, BUT ONE OF THE CONTAINERS HAD BEEN OPENED!
THEY COULD HAVE USED ME FOR LUCK!
THIS IS WEIRD!
A REAL MYSTERY!
?
I ABANDONED SHIP.
THERE WAS AN UNFINISHED MESSAGE IN THE CABIN!
I HAD A GREAT FALL!
ON DECEMBER 5, 1872 SHE WAS DISCOVERED 600 MILES FROM PORTUGAL IN THE MID-ATLANTIC.
THE SHIP WAS DESERTED.
I LOVE A MYSTERY.
THE LIFEBOAT WAS MISSING.
IFE AND DAUGHTER WITH HIM.
SOME OF THE SHIP'S SAILS WERE TORN AND THE SHIP LOOKED OUT OF CONTROL.
THE SHIP WAS ABANDONED QUICKLY!
I'M SICK OF THE SEA.
THIS WATER IS TOO WET FOR ME!
I'M A FALLEN STAR.
I'M A STAR-FISH!
I'M FAN MAIL!
T HIS

How Things Work

Search and find lots of interesting facts about:

- Hot-Air Balloon
- Light Bulb
- Submarine
- Making Paper
- Helicopter
- Orchestra
- Microwave Oven
- Human Heart
- Solar Energy
- Airplane
- Lasers

HOT-AIR BALLOON

A hot-air balloon achieves flight when the air inside the balloon is heated. Since the heated air inside is lighter than the cool air outside, the balloon rises toward the sky.

The first hot-air balloon to carry passengers was invented by the Montgolfier brothers in France in 1783. It flew about 5 miles.

See if you can find all the things you did or didn't know about hot-air balloons in this picture. Don't forget to look for the following fun things, too.

- ☐ Arrows (7)
- ☐ Bee
- ☐ Cactus
- ☐ Candle
- ☐ Carrot
- ☐ Dragon
- ☐ Duck
- ☐ Eye
- ☐ Fire hydrant
- ☐ First passenger balloon
- ☐ Fish
- ☐ Flowers
- ☐ Football
- ☐ Happy face
- ☐ Heart
- ☐ Humpty Dumpty
- ☐ Ice-cream cone
- ☐ Kite
- ☐ Light bulb
- ☐ Lips
- ☐ Moon face
- ☐ Paper airplane
- ☐ Pencil
- ☐ Star
- ☐ Superhero
- ☐ Teapot
- ☐ Tent
- ☐ Thermometer
- ☐ Top hat
- ☐ Umbrella

What is another name for the balloon?
How can the balloon move downward at a faster speed?

IN FLIGHT, THE PILOT CONTROLS THE HEIGHT OF THE BALLOON BY OCCASIONALLY TURNING ON THE BURNER.
BALLOONS HAVE NO ENGINES. THE DIRECTION IN WHICH THEY GO IS DETERMINED BY THE WIND!
THIS IS MY BALLOON
THE ENVELOPE CAN BE MADE OF ALMOST ANY SHAPE.
WE'RE GOING THAT WAY!
DON'T COME NEAR ME!
EYE SEE YOU!
TO DESCEND FASTER, A PORT OR HOLE AT THE TOP OF THE ENVELOPE IS OPENED.
I HOPE IT DOESN'T MELT!
JOSEPH AND JACQUES MONTGOLFIER, FRENCH BROTHERS, BUILT THE FIRST BALLOON THAT CARRIED PASSENGERS, IN 1783.
THAT'S 120 YEARS BEFOR THE WRIGHT BROTHERS BUILT THE FIRST AIRPLANE!
GOING DOWN.
I HOPE THAT BEE DOESN'T SEE US!
THE WORLD IS SO QUIET FROM UP HERE.
WHEN THE BURNER IS TURNED OFF, THE AIR TEMPERATURE IN THE BALLOON COOLS. THIS CAUSES THE ENVELOPE TO SHRINK, INCREASING THE WEIGHT OF THE BALLOON AND ALLOWING IT TO DESCEND OR FLOAT DOWNWARD.
I FORGOT THE MUSTARD!
WE'RE TAKING OFF!
I HAD A GREAT SPRING.
THE BALLOON IS BEING INFLATED WITH HOT AIR FROM THE BURNER TO INFLATE IT AND GET IT OFF THE GROUND.
WE HAVE TO FILL IT UP WITH HOT AIR.
IT'S SLOWLY FILLING WITH HOT AIR.
WHY DON'T YOU TALK TO IT, TOO? HA-HA-HA!
HAVE A GOOD TRIP.
OOOPS!

LIGHTEN UP EVERYBODY!
THE FILAMENT IS A TIGHTLY WOUND WIRE MADE OF TUNGSTEN METAL.
TUNGSTEN IS USED BECAUSE IT WON'T MELT WHEN THE ELECTRICITY HEATS IT UP. IT HAS A VERY HIGH MELTING POINT.
IS IT HALLOWEEN YET?
THE AIRTIGHT BULB IS FILLED WITH ARGON, AN INERT GAS.
AN INERT GAS IS A GAS THAT IS NOT ACTIVE AND WON'T CHEMICALLY COMBINE.
WITHOUT ARGO THE EXTREME HOT TUNGSTE FILAMENT WOU COMBINE WITH OXYGEN IN THE AIR AND BURN UP!
I'M NOT AFRAID OF THE DARK.
WE HAVE GREEN LIGHT BULBS ON MY PLANET.
I'M NOT PLUGGED IN.
THE GREATER THE RESISTAN THE HOTTER IT GETS AND THE BRIGHTER TH LIGHT!
WHEN YOU TURN THE LIGHT SWITCH ON, ELECTRICITY FLOWS THROUGH THE SWITCH TO THE CONTACTS ON THE BULB AND ON THROUGH THE FILAMENT.
THE THINNER THE FILAMENT WIRE, THE GREATER THE RESISTANCE.
THE FILAMENT WIRE RESISTS THE ELECTRIC CURRENT. WHEN THE RESISTANCE IS GREAT ENOUGH THE WIRE GLOWS WHITE HOT AND PRODUCES LIGHT!
THE FILAM REACH TEMPE OF A 4,50 DEGR
I DON'T GROW WELL IN THE DARK.
I LOOK GOOD IN THE DARK.
EVENTUALLY, THE HIGH HEAT CAUSES THE FILAMENT TO BREAK AND EVAPORATE. NOW THE BULB IS "BURNED OUT."
THE DARK COLOR THAT APPEARS IN THE BULB WHEN IT BURNS OUT IS REALLY A THIN FILM OF EVAPORATED TUNGSTEN THAT HAS COATED THE INNER SURFACE OF THE GLASS BULB.
"VOLTS" TELL HOW STRONG THE ELECTRIC CURRENT MUST BE FOR THE BULB TO WORK PROPERLY.
"WATTS" DETERMINE HOW MUCH ELECTRI CURRENT A BULB USES. THE GREATER THE WATTAGE THE BRIGHTER THE BUL
I DON'T WANT TO BE SEEN HERE.
WHAT?
THOMAS ALVA EDISON INVENTED THE LIGHT BULB.
THIS IS A PICTURE OF THE FIRST LIGHT BULB.
I DIDN'T KNOW THAT!
NOW I KNOW IT!
I'M LOST.

LIGHT BULB

An electric light bulb contains a filament, an inert gas, electrical contacts, and a glass bulb. Light is produced when an electric current passes through the filament. The current heats the filament to a temperature high enough to produce white light.

Thomas Edison invented the light bulb in 1879.

See if you can find all the things you did or didn't know about light bulbs in this picture. Don't forget to look for the following fun things, too.

- ☐ Alarm clock
- ☐ Apple
- ☐ Baby's bib
- ☐ Baseball bat
- ☐ Bone
- ☐ Burned-out bulb
- ☐ Candles (2)
- ☐ Clipboard
- ☐ Clown
- ☐ Crayon
- ☐ Elephant
- ☐ Envelope
- ☐ Fish (2)
- ☐ Flowers (2)
- ☐ Football
- ☐ Fork
- ☐ Ghost
- ☐ Heart
- ☐ Helmet
- ☐ Horse's head
- ☐ Horseshoe
- ☐ Hose
- ☐ Jump rope
- ☐ Necktie
- ☐ Paintbrush
- ☐ Paper bag
- ☐ Pencil
- ☐ Pizza box
- ☐ Saw
- ☐ Tepee
- ☐ Used tire
- ☐ Vest

What is a filament made of?
What determines the brightness of a light bulb?

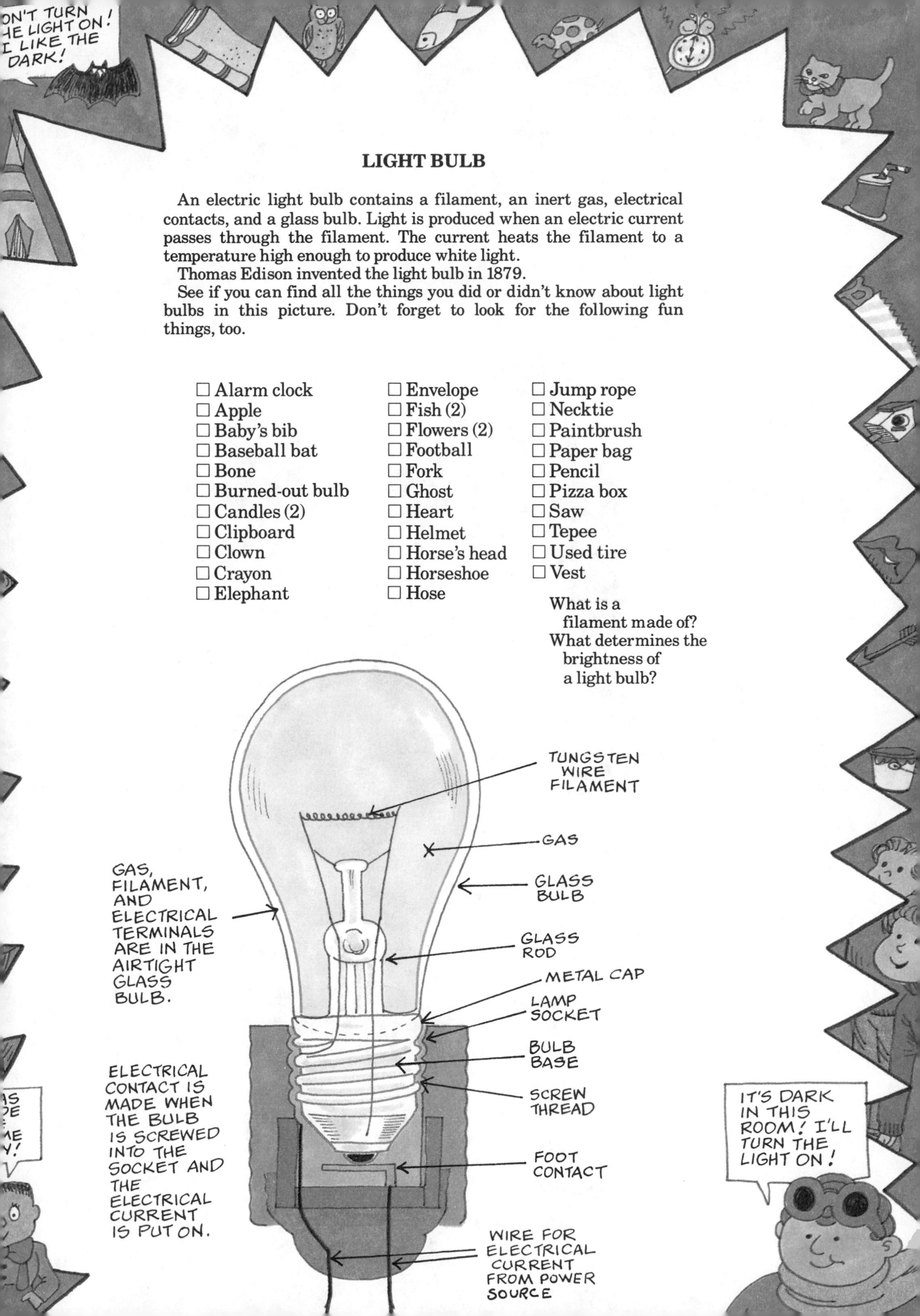

ON'T TURN
HE LIGHT ON!
I LIKE THE
DARK!
TUNGSTEN WIRE FILAMENT
GAS
GLASS BULB
GAS, FILAMENT, AND ELECTRICAL TERMINALS ARE IN THE AIRTIGHT GLASS BULB.
GLASS ROD
METAL CAP
LAMP SOCKET
BULB BASE
SCREW THREAD
ELECTRICAL CONTACT IS MADE WHEN THE BULB IS SCREWED INTO THE SOCKET AND THE ELECTRICAL CURRENT IS PUT ON.
FOOT CONTACT
WIRE FOR ELECTRICAL CURRENT FROM POWER SOURCE
IT'S DARK IN THIS ROOM! I'LL TURN THE LIGHT ON!

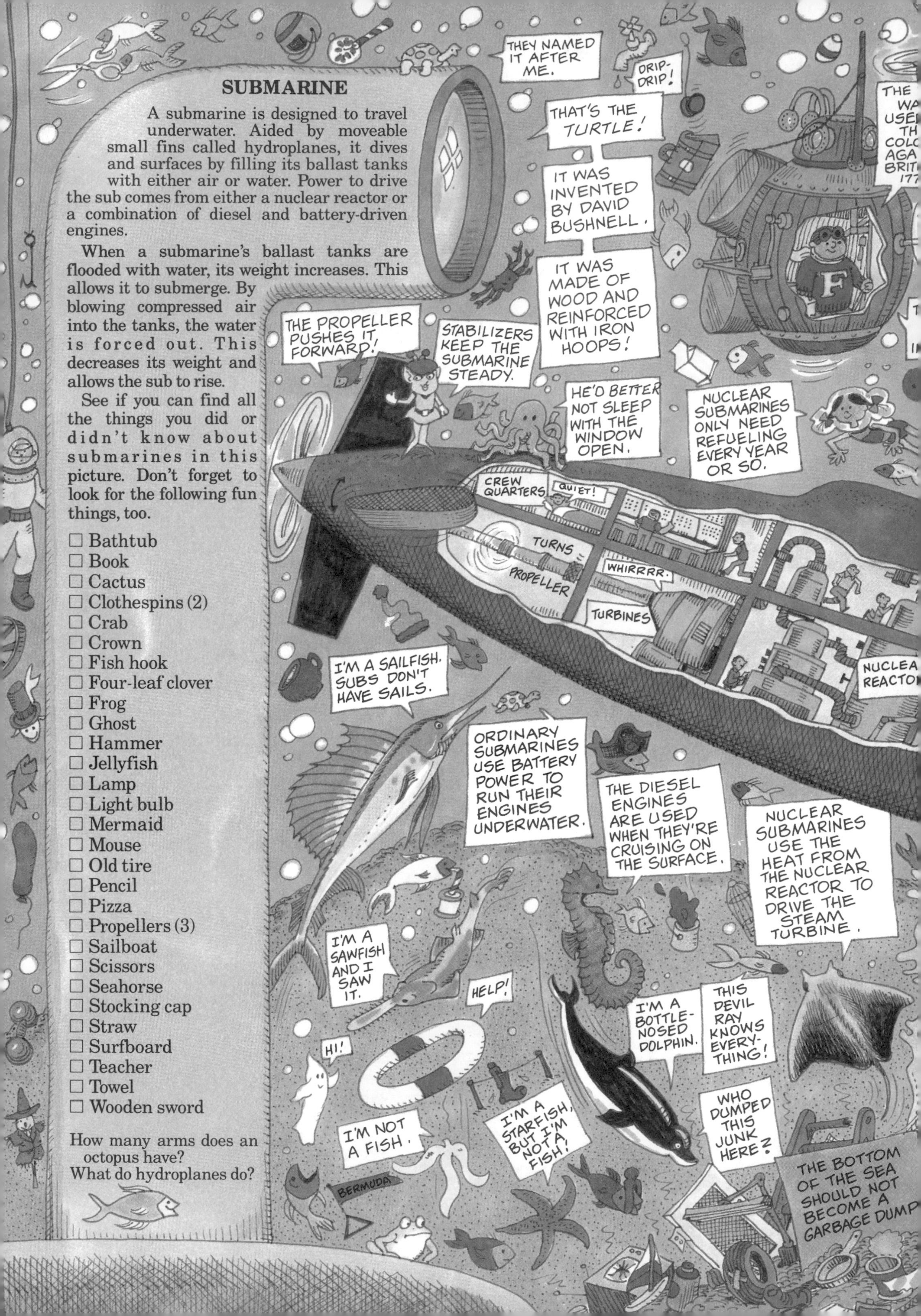

SUBMARINE

A submarine is designed to travel underwater. Aided by moveable small fins called hydroplanes, it dives and surfaces by filling its ballast tanks with either air or water. Power to drive the sub comes from either a nuclear reactor or a combination of diesel and battery-driven engines.

When a submarine's ballast tanks are flooded with water, its weight increases. This allows it to submerge. By blowing compressed air into the tanks, the water is forced out. This decreases its weight and allows the sub to rise.

See if you can find all the things you did or didn't know about submarines in this picture. Don't forget to look for the following fun things, too.

- ☐ Bathtub
- ☐ Book
- ☐ Cactus
- ☐ Clothespins (2)
- ☐ Crab
- ☐ Crown
- ☐ Fish hook
- ☐ Four-leaf clover
- ☐ Frog
- ☐ Ghost
- ☐ Hammer
- ☐ Jellyfish
- ☐ Lamp
- ☐ Light bulb
- ☐ Mermaid
- ☐ Mouse
- ☐ Old tire
- ☐ Pencil
- ☐ Pizza
- ☐ Propellers (3)
- ☐ Sailboat
- ☐ Scissors
- ☐ Seahorse
- ☐ Stocking cap
- ☐ Straw
- ☐ Surfboard
- ☐ Teacher
- ☐ Towel
- ☐ Wooden sword

How many arms does an octopus have?
What do hydroplanes do?

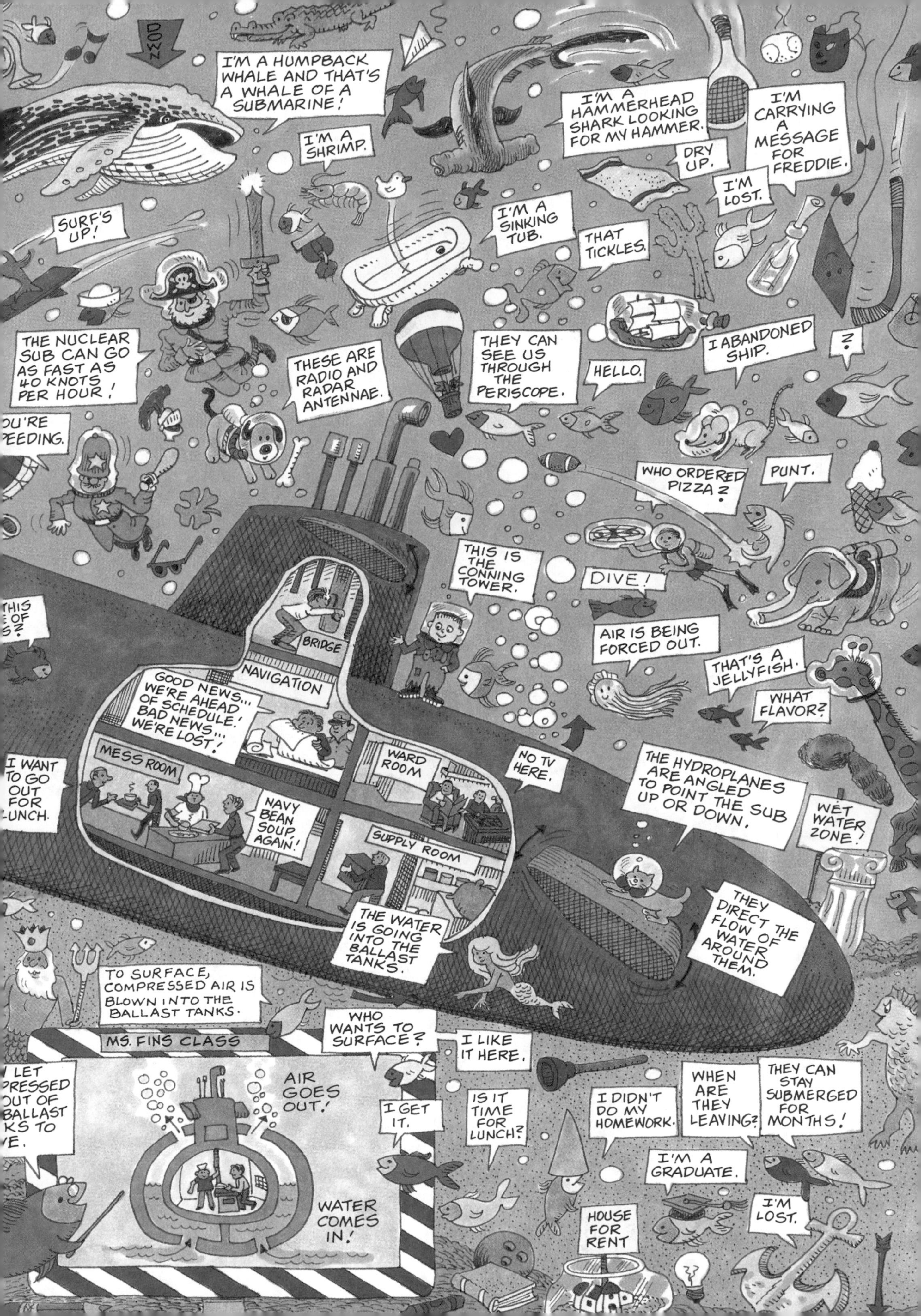

DOWN
I'M A HUMPBACK WHALE AND THAT'S A WHALE OF A SUBMARINE!
I'M A SHRIMP.
I'M A HAMMERHEAD SHARK LOOKING FOR MY HAMMER.
DRY UP.
I'M CARRYING A MESSAGE FOR FREDDIE.
I'M LOST.
SURF'S UP!
I'M A SINKING TUB.
THAT TICKLES.
THE NUCLEAR SUB CAN GO AS FAST AS 40 KNOTS PER HOUR!
THESE ARE RADIO AND RADAR ANTENNAE.
THEY CAN SEE US THROUGH THE PERISCOPE.
HELLO.
I ABANDONED SHIP.
?
OU'RE PEEDING.
WHO ORDERED PIZZA?
PUNT.
THIS IS THE CONNING TOWER.
DIVE!
THIS
E OF
S?
AIR IS BEING FORCED OUT.
THAT'S A JELLYFISH.
WHAT FLAVOR?
BRIDGE
NAVIGATION
GOOD NEWS... WE'RE AHEAD OF SCHEDULE! BAD NEWS... WE'RE LOST!
MESS ROOM
WARD ROOM
NO TV HERE.
I WANT TO GO OUT FOR LUNCH.
NAVY BEAN SOUP AGAIN!
SUPPLY ROOM
THE HYDROPLANES ARE ANGLED TO POINT THE SUB UP OR DOWN.
WET WATER ZONE!
THEY DIRECT THE FLOW OF WATER AROUND THEM.
THE WATER IS GOING INTO THE BALLAST TANKS.
TO SURFACE, COMPRESSED AIR IS BLOWN INTO THE BALLAST TANKS.
MS. FINS CLASS
WHO WANTS TO SURFACE?
I LIKE IT HERE.
LET
PRESSED
OUT OF
BALLAST
KS TO
E.
AIR GOES OUT!
WATER COMES IN!
I GET IT.
IS IT TIME FOR LUNCH?
I DIDN'T DO MY HOMEWORK.
WHEN ARE THEY LEAVING?
THEY CAN STAY SUBMERGED FOR MONTHS!
I'M A GRADUATE.
HOUSE FOR RENT
I'M LOST.

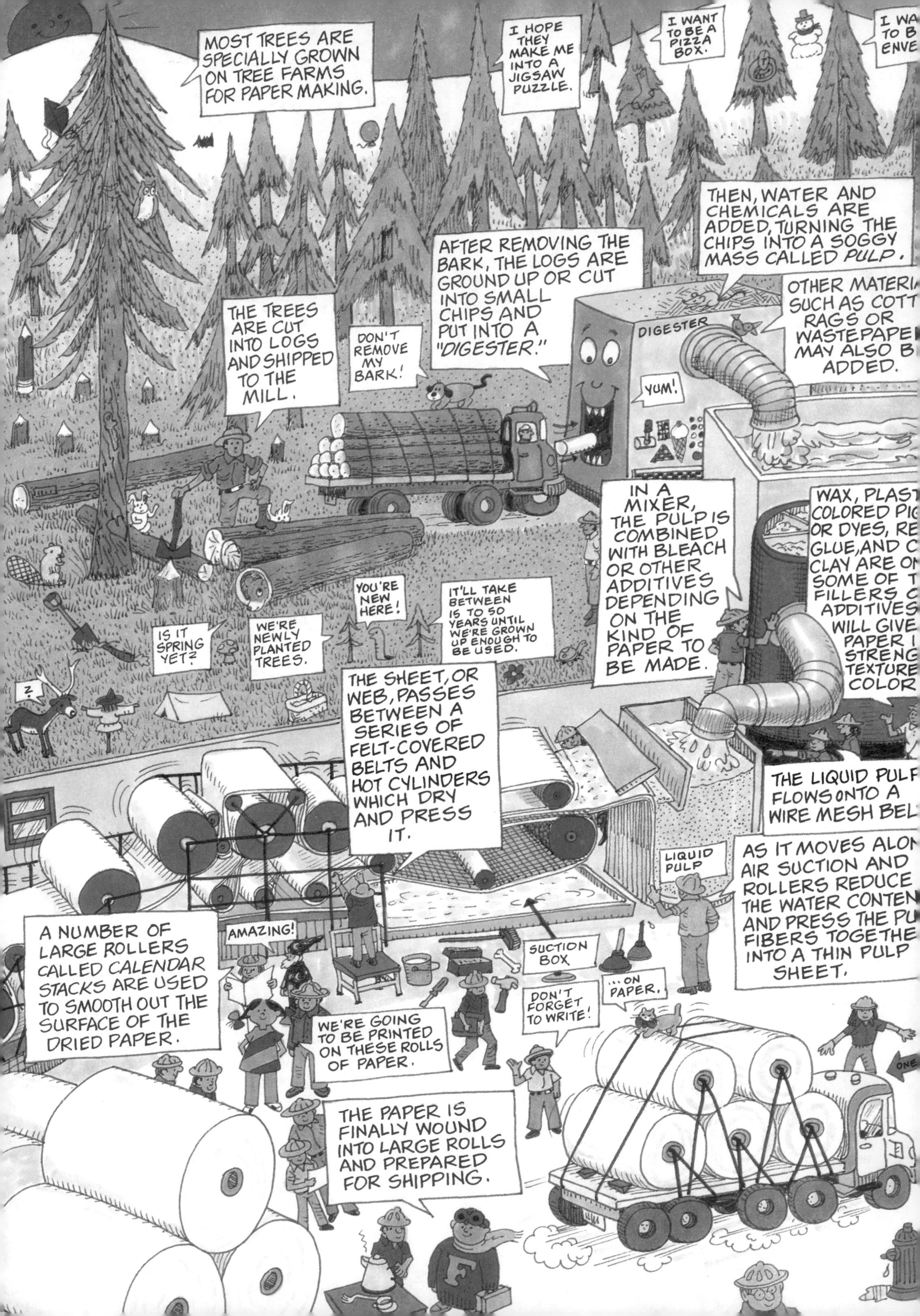

MOST TREES ARE SPECIALLY GROWN ON TREE FARMS FOR PAPER MAKING.
I HOPE THEY MAKE ME INTO A JIGSAW PUZZLE.
I WANT TO BE A PIZZA BOX.
I WA TO B ENVE
THE TREES ARE CUT INTO LOGS AND SHIPPED TO THE MILL.
DON'T REMOVE MY BARK!
AFTER REMOVING THE BARK, THE LOGS ARE GROUND UP OR CUT INTO SMALL CHIPS AND PUT INTO A "DIGESTER."
THEN, WATER AND CHEMICALS ARE ADDED, TURNING THE CHIPS INTO A SOGGY MASS CALLED PULP.
DIGESTER
YUM!
OTHER MATERI SUCH AS COTT RAGS OR WASTEPAPE MAY ALSO B ADDED.
IN A MIXER, THE PULP IS COMBINED WITH BLEACH OR OTHER ADDITIVES DEPENDING ON THE KIND OF PAPER TO BE MADE.
WAX, PLAST COLORED PIG OR DYES, RE GLUE, AND C CLAY ARE ON SOME OF T FILLERS O ADDITIVES WILL GIVE PAPER I STRENG TEXTURE COLOR
IS IT SPRING YET?
WE'RE NEWLY PLANTED TREES.
YOU'RE NEW HERE!
IT'LL TAKE BETWEEN 15 TO 50 YEARS UNTIL WE'RE GROWN UP ENOUGH TO BE USED.
Z
THE SHEET, OR WEB, PASSES BETWEEN A SERIES OF FELT-COVERED BELTS AND HOT CYLINDERS WHICH DRY AND PRESS IT.
THE LIQUID PULP FLOWS ONTO A WIRE MESH BEL
LIQUID PULP
AS IT MOVES ALON AIR SUCTION AND ROLLERS REDUCE THE WATER CONTEN AND PRESS THE PU FIBERS TOGETHE INTO A THIN PULP SHEET.
SUCTION BOX
A NUMBER OF LARGE ROLLERS CALLED CALENDAR STACKS ARE USED TO SMOOTH OUT THE SURFACE OF THE DRIED PAPER.
AMAZING!
WE'RE GOING TO BE PRINTED ON THESE ROLLS OF PAPER.
DON'T FORGET TO WRITE!
...ON PAPER.
THE PAPER IS FINALLY WOUND INTO LARGE ROLLS AND PREPARED FOR SHIPPING.
ONE
F

MAKING PAPER

About 5,000 years ago, the Egyptians used a writing material made from a plant called papyrus. Today, from soft tissues to tough cardboard, paper is made chiefly from fibers produced by trees, in large factories called paper mills.

See if you can find all the things you did or didn't know about making paper in this picture. Don't forget to look for the following fun things, too.

- ☐ Balloon
- ☐ Basket
- ☐ Bear
- ☐ Bird
- ☐ Bow and arrow
- ☐ Broom
- ☐ Bucket
- ☐ Cane
- ☐ Carrot
- ☐ Fish
- ☐ Flower
- ☐ Fork
- ☐ Heart
- ☐ Ice-cream cone
- ☐ Key
- ☐ Kite
- ☐ Mouse
- ☐ Mushroom
- ☐ Oil can
- ☐ Owl
- ☐ Paper airplane
- ☐ Plumber's helper
- ☐ Ring
- ☐ Shopping bag
- ☐ Skier
- ☐ Snowman
- ☐ Telescope
- ☐ Toothbrush
- ☐ Turtles (2)
- ☐ Wizard
- ☐ Worm

What are calendar stacks?

Who invented the kind of paper that we use today?

HELICOPTER

Helicopters can fly straight up or down, forward or backward, sideways, and even hover in place. Because of their mobility they can fly into places that airplanes cannot.

The first helicopter to achieve flight was built in France in 1907. But it was not completely reliable. In 1939, Igor Sikorsky developed the first successful one and the modern era of helicopters began.

See if you can find all the things you did or didn't know about helicopters in this picture. Don't forget to look for the following fun things, too.

- ☐ Balloon
- ☐ Bee
- ☐ Book
- ☐ Butterfly
- ☐ Cactus
- ☐ Camera
- ☐ Candy cane
- ☐ Canteen
- ☐ Flying bat
- ☐ Frog
- ☐ Heart
- ☐ Jack-o'-lantern
- ☐ Lollipop
- ☐ Medal
- ☐ Mouse
- ☐ Oil can
- ☐ Owl
- ☐ Pail
- ☐ Paper airplane
- ☐ Penguin
- ☐ Periscope
- ☐ Roller skates
- ☐ Sailboat
- ☐ Schoolbag
- ☐ Screwdriver
- ☐ Squirrel
- ☐ Tennis racket
- ☐ Turtle
- ☐ Worm

How many main rotor blades do most helicopters have?
What gives a helicopter its power?

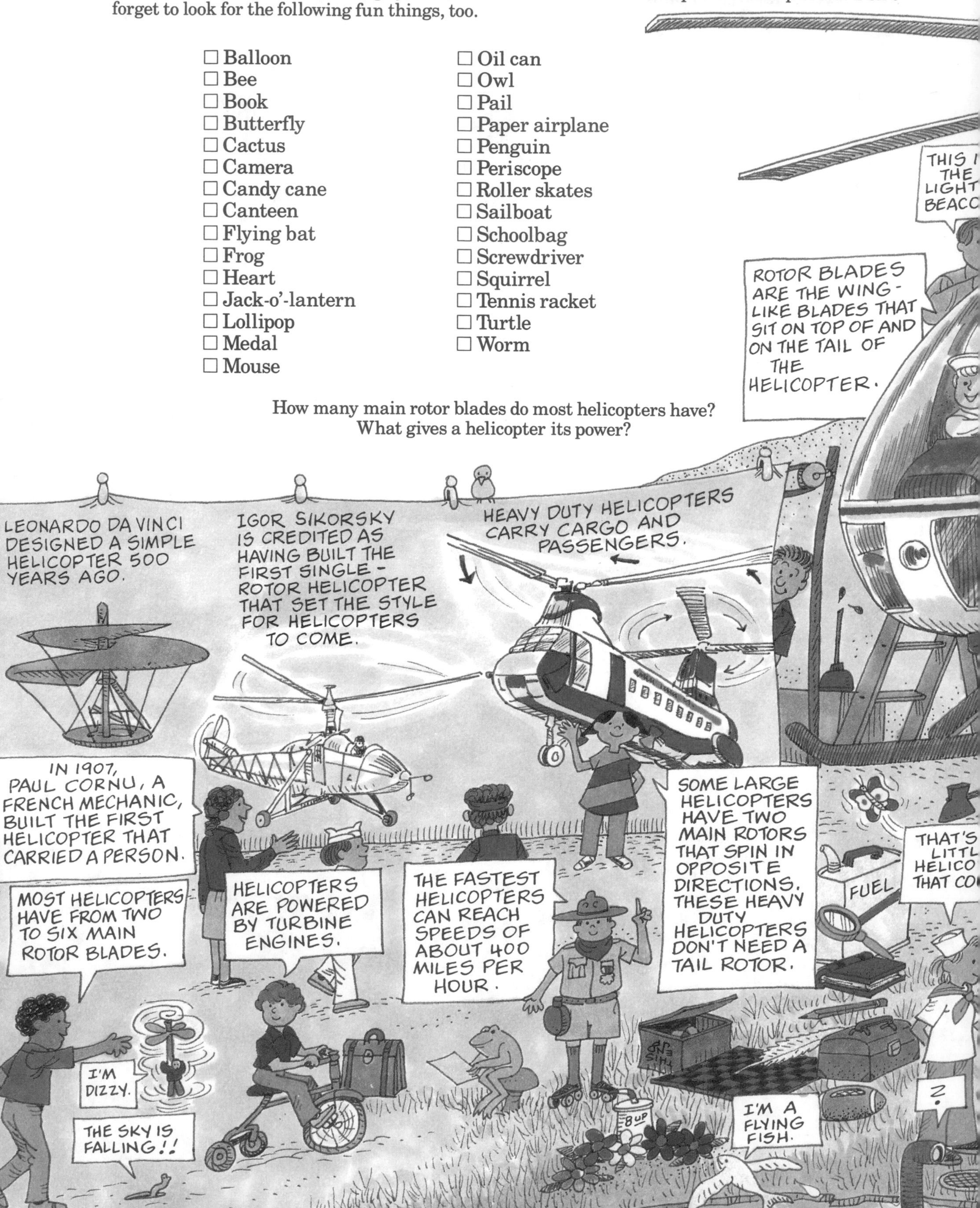

I WONDER HOW I WORK?
I CAN'T HOVER.
I'D LIKE TO HOVER.
HELICOPTERS CAN LAND IN PLACES OTHER VEHICLES CAN'T GET TO.
THIS IS THE MAIN ROTOR.
I CAN GET THERE.
I THINK I CAN'T... I KNOW I CAN'T!
HOW DO WE GET UP THERE?
THE MAIN ROTOR BLADES ARE ATTACHED TO A ROTOR SHAFT THAT GOES THROUGH THE ROOF AND CONNECTS TO THE ENGINE.
THIS IS THE TAIL ROTOR.
THE ENGINE TURNS THE SHAFT MAKING THE BLADES WHIRL LIKE PROPELLERS.
THE TAIL ROTOR HELPS BALANCE THE HELICOPTER AND KEEPS IT FROM SPINNING OUT OF CONTROL.
BY CONTROLLING THE PITCH OF THE TAIL ROTOR WITH A PEDAL, THE PILOT CAN TURN THE HELICOPTER LEFT OR RIGHT.
THE TAIL AND FINS KEEP THE HELICOPTER STABLE AS IT FLIES.
THE PILOT CAN CHANGE THE FLIGHT DIRECTION OF THE HELICOPTER BY TILTING THE MAIN ROTOR AND ALTERING THE ANGLE, OR PITCH, OF THE BLADES.
THE HELICOPTER HAS LANDED.
DO I REALLY LOOK LIKE A PILOT?
THE PILOT CONTROLS THE FLIGHT WITH TWO *PITCH STICKS*.
OVING ONE PITCH
IN THESE
CTIONS, THE PILOT
THE MAIN ROTOR
DES AND THE
COPTER WILL FLY
NY DIRECTION.
ANOTHER STICK RAISES AND LOWERS THE CRAFT TO GO UP, DOWN, OR HOVER!
I DIDN'T KNOW, THAT!
I KNOW IT NOW!
ME, TOO!
ARD - ROTOR BLADES TILTED FORWARD
BACKWARD - ROTOR BLADES TILTED BACKWARD
OWN·HOVERING -
SIDEWAYS - ROTOR BLADES TILTED IN DIRECTION OF TRAVEL
LADES
TCH
PENGUINS DON'T FLY!
NEITHER DO I!

ORCHESTRA

An orchestra is not a random gathering of musicians and their instruments. It is a carefully planned group of different types of instruments with each one having its own part to play in the performance.

See if you can find all the things you did or didn't know about orchestras in this picture. Don't forget to look for the following fun things, too.

- ☐ Ball of string
- ☐ Balloon
- ☐ Baseball cap
- ☐ Bird
- ☐ Broom
- ☐ Brush
- ☐ Candle
- ☐ Cast
- ☐ Duck

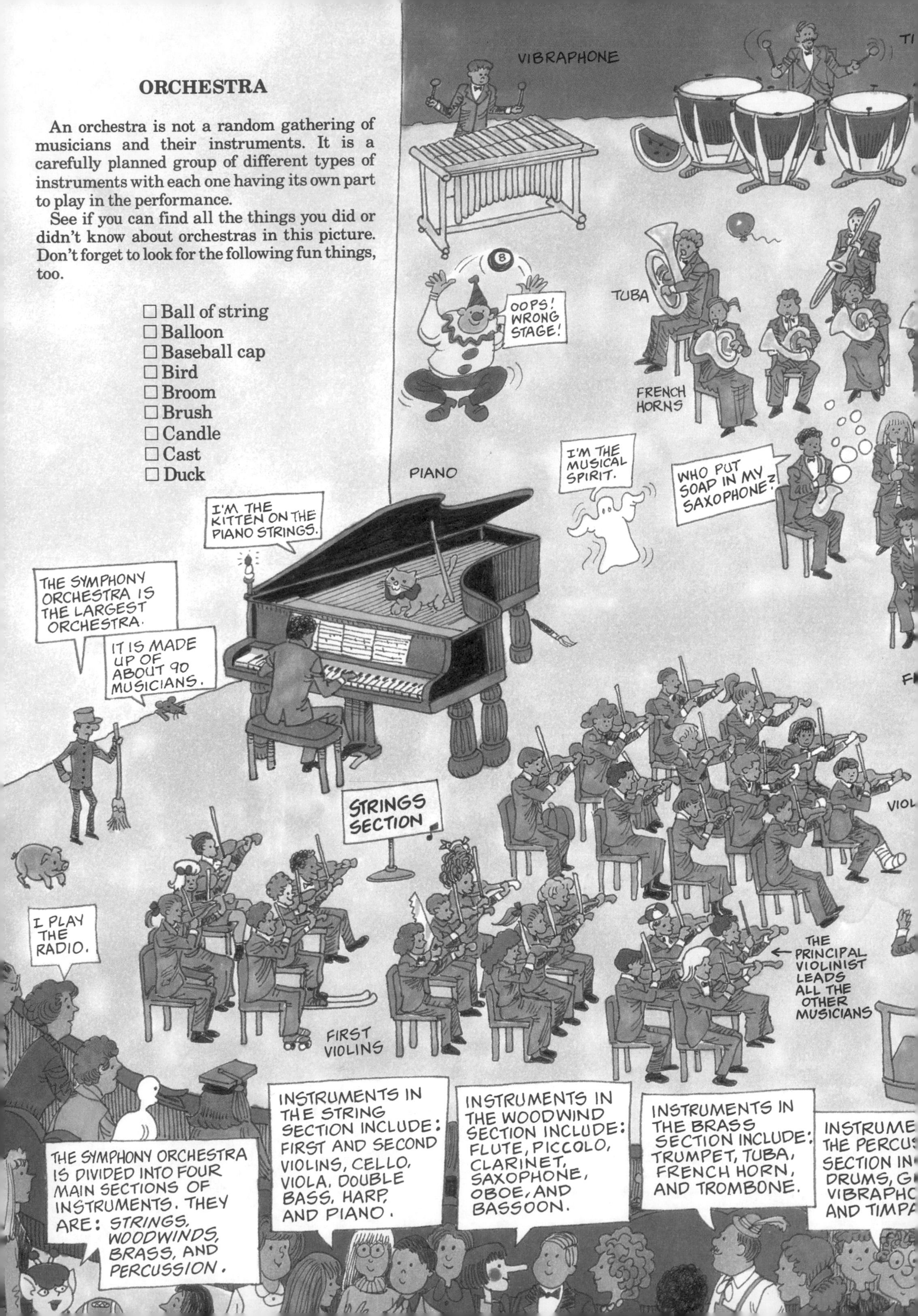

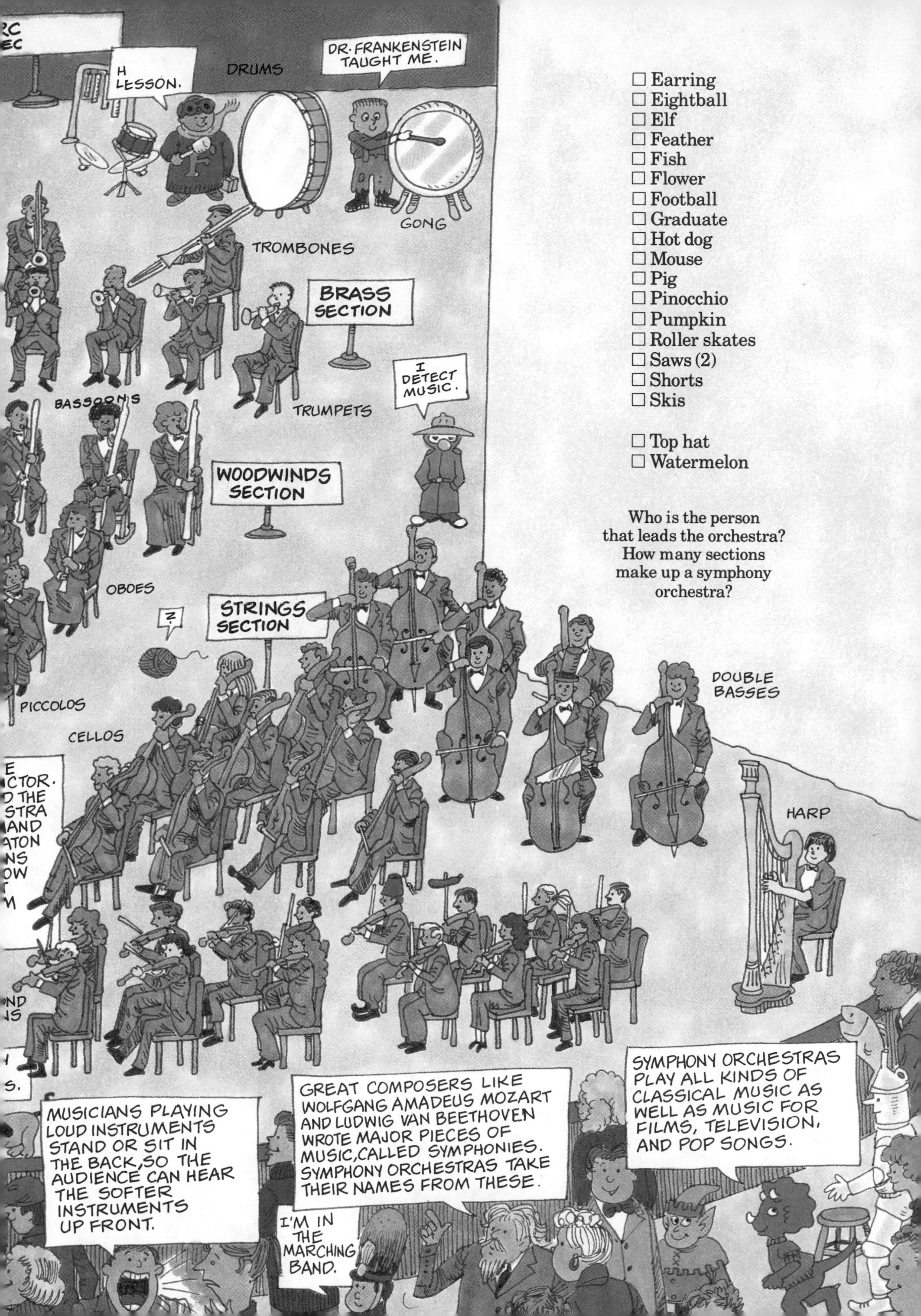

- ☐ Earring
- ☐ Eightball
- ☐ Elf
- ☐ Feather
- ☐ Fish
- ☐ Flower
- ☐ Football
- ☐ Graduate
- ☐ Hot dog
- ☐ Mouse
- ☐ Pig
- ☐ Pinocchio
- ☐ Pumpkin
- ☐ Roller skates
- ☐ Saws (2)
- ☐ Shorts
- ☐ Skis

- ☐ Top hat
- ☐ Watermelon

Who is the person that leads the orchestra? How many sections make up a symphony orchestra?

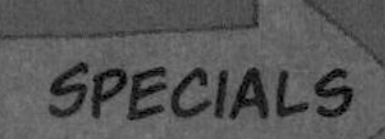

MICROWAVE OVEN

Microwaves are waves of invisible heat energy. Unlike ordinary ovens that use gas or electric heat, a microwave oven uses microwaves to heat, defrost, and cook food.

See if you can find all the things you did or didn't know about microwaves in this picture. Don't forget to look for the following fun things, too.

- ☐ Ball
- ☐ Ballerina
- ☐ Bone
- ☐ Book
- ☐ Bottle
- ☐ Cane
- ☐ Cape
- ☐ Chef's hat
- ☐ Deer
- ☐ Elf
- ☐ Fan
- ☐ Football helmet
- ☐ Fork
- ☐ Hard hat
- ☐ Knife
- ☐ Lion
- ☐ Moose
- ☐ Mouse
- ☐ Napkin holder
- ☐ Necktie
- ☐ Olive
- ☐ Owl
- ☐ Pizza
- ☐ Santa Claus
- ☐ Shark fin
- ☐ Straw
- ☐ Tinman
- ☐ Top hat
- ☐ Turtle
- ☐ Wristwatch

How do microwaves cook food?
Why shouldn't metal containers be used in microwave ovens?

URGER
HOT HAMBURGER WITH ALL THE FIXINGS
MUST SHOW PROOF OF AGE. SERVED ONLY TO UNDER SIXTEEN YEAR OLDS.
HOT COCOA
HOT PIE
HOT SOUP OF THE DAY
HOT RIBS/ CHICKEN
IT TASTES GOOD.
I'M TOO OLD.
HO-HO-HOT!
I'M IN A BIG HURRY!
I BROUGHT MY OWN FROZEN PIZZA TO HEAT UP.
"NUKE" ME!
THERE'S A HARE IN THE SOUP!
I DON'T KNOW WHAT TO ORDER!
I'M GOING TO EAT THIS BY MYSELF!
MY BONE IS COLD.
MENU
I FORGOT THE HAMBURGER
WE SERVE EVERYBODY!
IS IT HOT YET?
IN A MICROWAVE
COOKS MANY
S FASTER BECAUSE
VAVES PENETRATING
FOOD HEAT IT FROM
INSIDE OUT
WELL AS FROM
OUTSIDE IN.
SPINNING REFLECTOR FAN
MICROWAVE BEAM
MICROWAVES
MAGNETRON
FOOD
CONTROLS
TURNTABLE

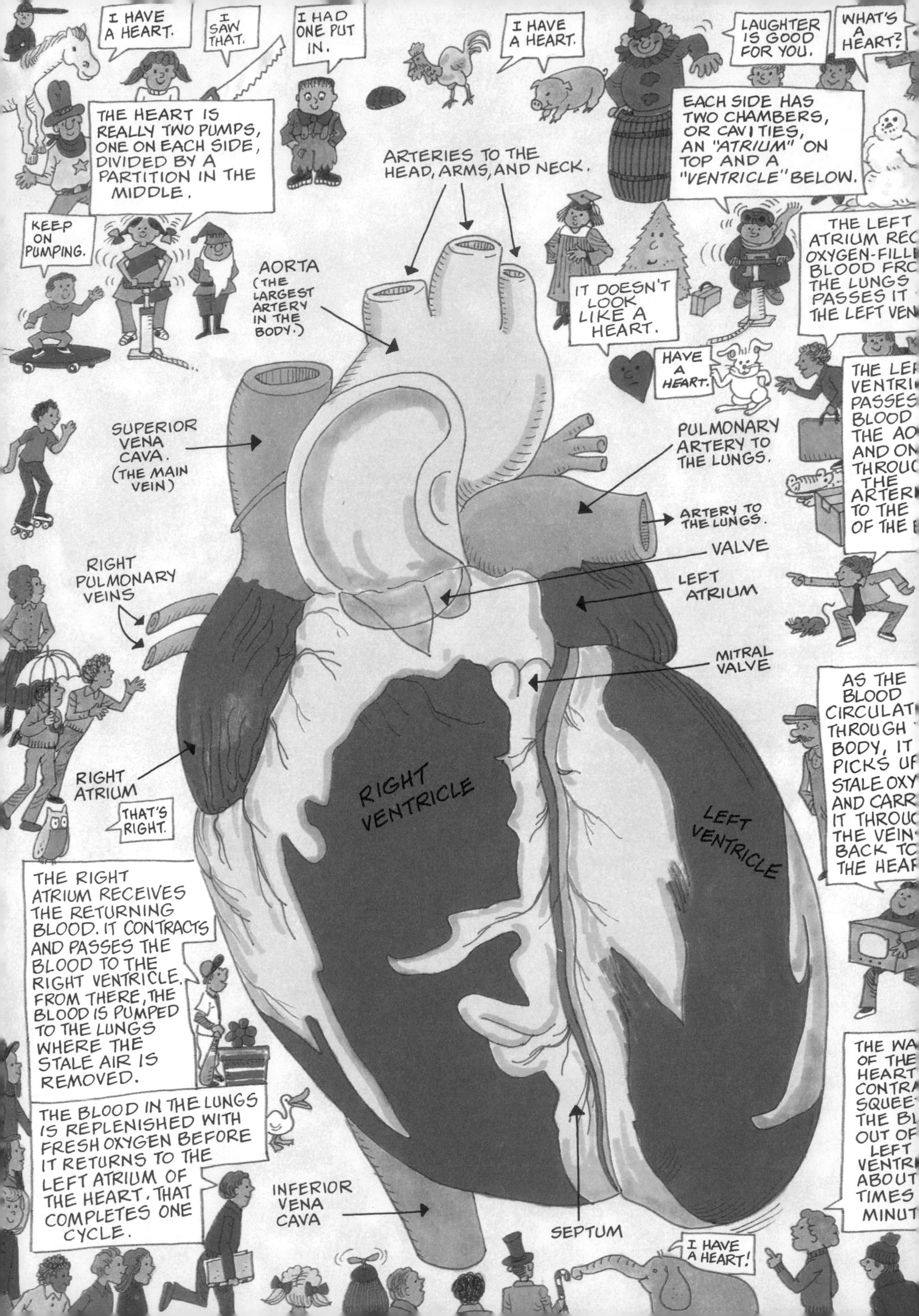

I HAVE A HEART.
I SAW THAT.
I HAD ONE PUT IN.
I HAVE A HEART.
LAUGHTER IS GOOD FOR YOU.
WHAT'S A HEART?
THE HEART IS REALLY TWO PUMPS, ONE ON EACH SIDE, DIVIDED BY A PARTITION IN THE MIDDLE.
EACH SIDE HAS TWO CHAMBERS, OR CAVITIES, AN "ATRIUM" ON TOP AND A "VENTRICLE" BELOW.
KEEP ON PUMPING.
ARTERIES TO THE HEAD, ARMS, AND NECK.
AORTA (THE LARGEST ARTERY IN THE BODY.)
IT DOESN'T LOOK LIKE A HEART.
THE LEFT ATRIUM REC
OXYGEN-FILLE
BLOOD FRO
THE LUNGS
PASSES IT
THE LEFT VEN
HAVE A HEART.
THE LEF
VENTRI
PASSES
BLOOD
THE AO
AND ON
THROU
THE
ARTER
TO THE
OF THE
SUPERIOR VENA CAVA. (THE MAIN VEIN)
PULMONARY ARTERY TO THE LUNGS.
ARTERY TO THE LUNGS.
VALVE
RIGHT PULMONARY VEINS
LEFT ATRIUM
MITRAL VALVE
AS THE
BLOOD
CIRCULAT
THROUGH
BODY, IT
PICKS UP
STALE OXY
AND CARR
IT THROUG
THE VEIN
BACK TO
THE HEAR
RIGHT ATRIUM
THAT'S RIGHT.
RIGHT VENTRICLE
LEFT VENTRICLE
THE RIGHT ATRIUM RECEIVES THE RETURNING BLOOD. IT CONTRACTS AND PASSES THE BLOOD TO THE RIGHT VENTRICLE. FROM THERE, THE BLOOD IS PUMPED TO THE LUNGS WHERE THE STALE AIR IS REMOVED.
THE BLOOD IN THE LUNGS IS REPLENISHED WITH FRESH OXYGEN BEFORE IT RETURNS TO THE LEFT ATRIUM OF THE HEART. THAT COMPLETES ONE CYCLE.
INFERIOR VENA CAVA
SEPTUM
THE WA
OF THE
HEART
CONTRA
SQUEE
THE B
OUT OF
LEFT
VENTR
ABOUT
TIMES
MINUT
I HAVE A HEART!

HUMAN HEART

A heart is a muscular pump that circulates blood through the blood vessels. The blood carries nourishment and oxygen to every part of the body. In one year the human heart pumps about 650,000 gallons of blood, enough to fill 50 swimming pools!

See if you can find all the things you did or didn't know about the human heart in this picture. Don't forget to look for the following fun things, too.

- ☐ Ball
- ☐ Banana peel
- ☐ Barrel
- ☐ Baseball bat
- ☐ Book
- ☐ Broom
- ☐ Candy cane
- ☐ Chicken
- ☐ Dracula
- ☐ Drum
- ☐ Duck
- ☐ Fish
- ☐ Flower
- ☐ Joggers (2)
- ☐ Lion
- ☐ Microscope
- ☐ Mouse
- ☐ Moustache
- ☐ Owl
- ☐ Pillow
- ☐ Propeller
- ☐ Roller skates
- ☐ Saw
- ☐ Singer
- ☐ Skateboard
- ☐ Stars (2)
- ☐ Top hat
- ☐ TV set
- ☐ Umbrella
- ☐ Worm

What are the heart's chambers called?

Approximately how long does it take for the blood to travel throughout the body?

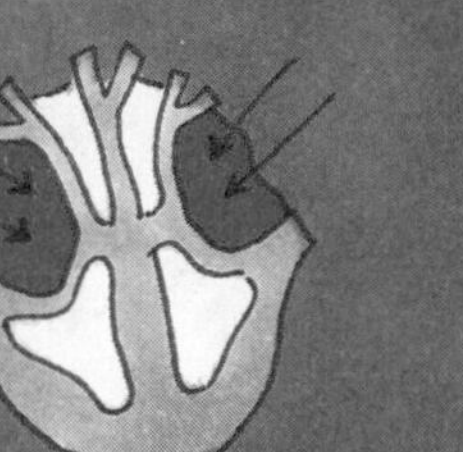

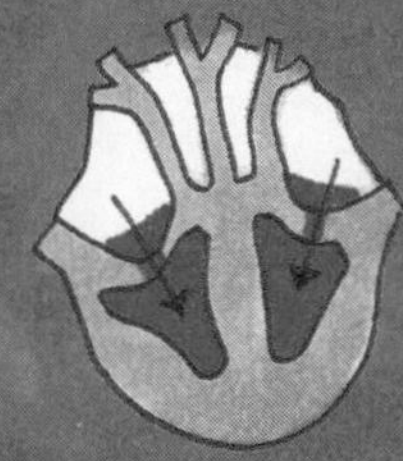

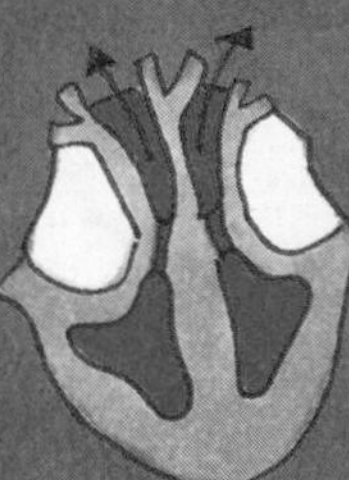

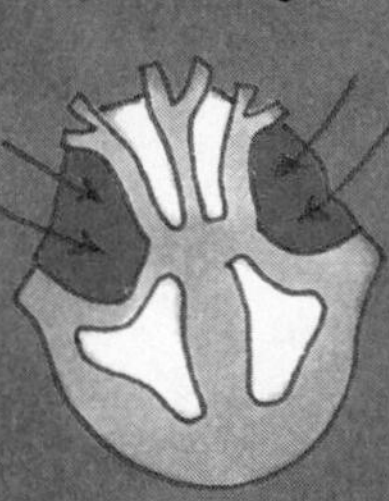

SOLAR ENERGY

Solar energy is power produced by the sun. It can be used to heat and purify water, give power to engines, and produce electricity. Five hundred and fifty billion tons of coal would have to be burned in order to equal the amount of solar energy received by the earth in only one day!

See if you can find all the things you did or didn't know about solar power in this picture. Don't forget to look for the following fun things, too.

- ☐ Apple
- ☐ Arrow
- ☐ Baseball
- ☐ Basketball hoop
- ☐ Bone
- ☐ Brush
- ☐ Buckets (2)
- ☐ Doghouse
- ☐ Duck
- ☐ Earmuffs
- ☐ Fire hydrant
- ☐ Flower
- ☐ Football
- ☐ Ghost
- ☐ Hammer
- ☐ Heart
- ☐ Helmet
- ☐ Kite
- ☐ Mailbox
- ☐ Newspaper
- ☐ Rabbit
- ☐ Screwdriver
- ☐ Star
- ☐ Tepee
- ☐ Turtle
- ☐ Umbrella
- ☐ Umpire
- ☐ Watering can
- ☐ Worm

What is solar power most commonly used for?
Why are the insides of solar panels painted black?

WHICH MOVES FASTER, HEAT OR COLD?
ONE OF THE MOST COMMON USES OF SOLAR POWER IS TO HEAT HOUSES.
SOLAR PANELS ARE USED TO COLLECT THE SUN'S RAYS AND TURN THEM INTO HEAT.
THEY WORK LIKE A GREENHOUSE. GLASS SHEETS COVER THE PANELS, TRAPPING THE SUN'S RAYS BY ALLOWING THEM IN, BUT NOT OUT!
ALUMINUM FOIL REFLECTS HEAT RAYS.
OOPS!
I MIGHT BE OUT OF A JOB.
I FLY SOUTH FOR THE WINTER.
COOL WATER IS PUMPED THROUGH COPPER TUBING IN THE PANELS. THE COPPER ABSORBS THE HEAT AND PASSES IT TO THE WATER.
HEATED WATER FLOWS TO A HOT WATER TANK.
THE HOT WATER TANK IS INSULATED IN ORDER TO KEEP THE WATER HOT!
A WATER PUMP IS USED TO CIRCULATE THE WATER THROUGH THE SOLAR PANELS.
DO YOU HAVE A CARROT?
WINDOWS ARE A PANE!

Y FAVORITE ISH IS THE SUNFISH!
AT NIGHT IT'S HE STARFISH.
THE SUN IS HOT!
SOLAR POWER IS A FREE SOURCE OF ENERGY!
AR POWER A GOOD A. I'M NG TO HAVE AT DONE, TOO.
EXPERIMENTAL CARS LIKE THIS HAVE BEEN BUILT TO RUN ON SOLAR POWER.
YOU'RE STILL GETTING A SPEEDING TICKET.
I'M NOT GETTING WET!
IT'S NOT RAINING!
SOLAR CELLS ARE ELECTRONIC DEVICES THAT CHANGE SUNLIGHT INTO ENERGY!
OH-OH!
RUN HOME!
THE HEAT IS TRAPPED IN THE WATER.
A COAT OF PAINT!
?
WARM WATER
SUN'S RAYS
USE FOR HEAT AND HOT WATER
INSULATED WATER STORAGE TANK
GLASS COVER
SOLAR POWER
BLACK MATERIAL TO ABSORB HEAT
ALUMINUM FOIL REFLECTS HEAT RAYS
SO, THAT'S HOW IT WORKS!
I DIDN'T KNOW THAT!
I KNOW IT NOW!
WATER PUMP
COOL WATER
COPPER TUBING
SOLAR PANEL.
F
I KNEW THAT ALL THE TIME.

AIRPLANE

Airplanes are fascinating pieces of machinery that soar through the air. Whether passenger, private, or military, they all operate under the same aerodynamic principles.

The first power-driven flight was made by the Wright brothers at Kitty Hawk, North Carolina in 1903.

See if you can find all the things you did or didn't know about airplanes in this picture. Don't forget to look for the following fun things, too.

- ☐ "X-1"
- ☐ Acrobat
- ☐ Banana
- ☐ Bowling ball
- ☐ Broom
- ☐ Elephant
- ☐ Fishing pole
- ☐ Flowers (3)
- ☐ Flying carpet
- ☐ Flying horse
- ☐ Flying saucer
- ☐ Football
- ☐ Ghost
- ☐ Glider
- ☐ Hamburger
- ☐ Hang glider
- ☐ Kite
- ☐ Mouse
- ☐ Paper airplane
- ☐ Pencil
- ☐ Pinwheel
- ☐ Pizza
- ☐ Sailboat
- ☐ Seaplane
- ☐ Sled
- ☐ Stars (2)
- ☐ Superheroes (2)
- ☐ Surfboard
- ☐ Turtle
- ☐ Umbrella
- ☐ Yo-yo

What provides an airplane's lift?
What kind of engine "pulls"
the airplane through the air?

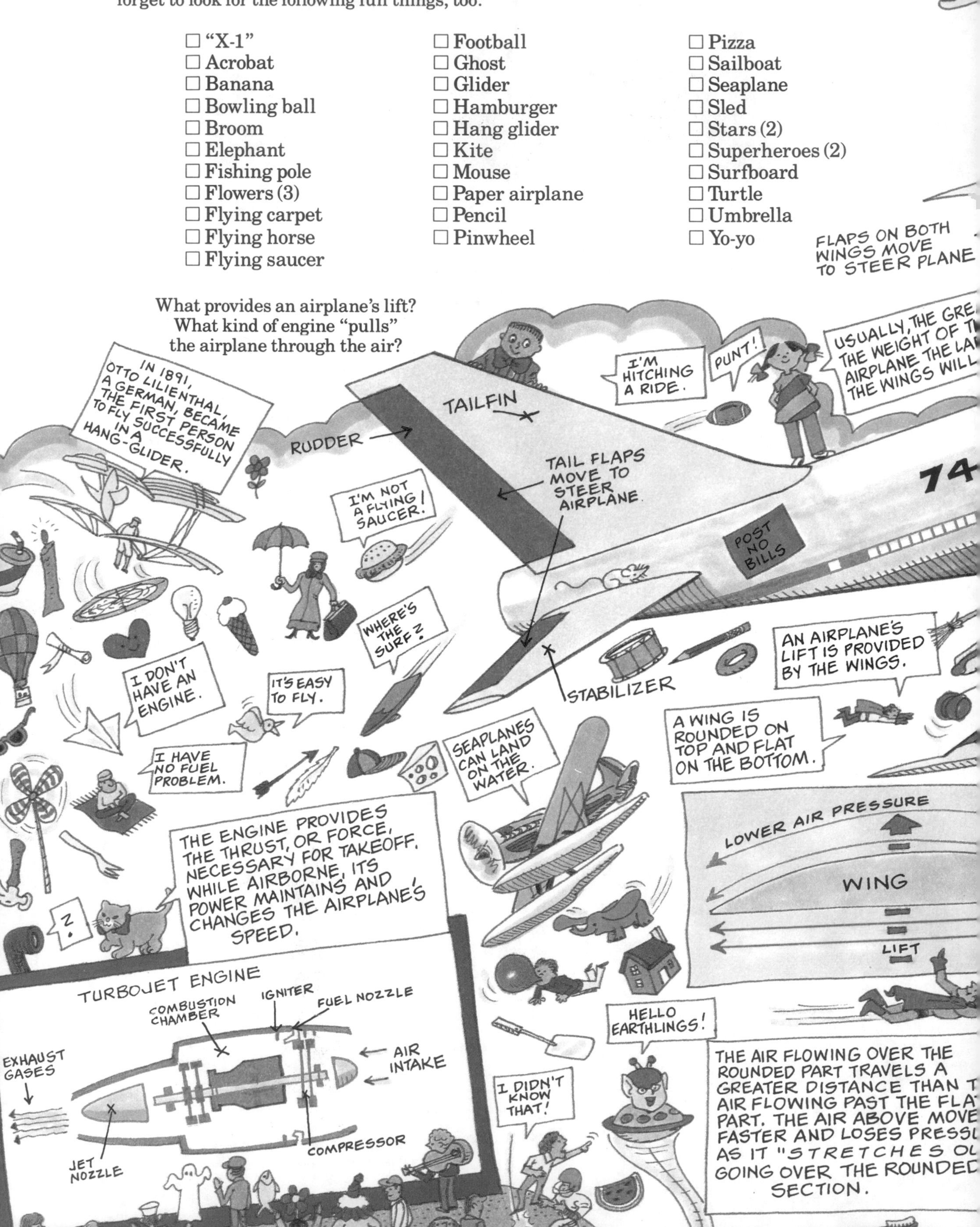

I'M A DC-3 PASSENGER AIRPLANE THAT WAS FLOWN IN 1943.
747 SEATING LAYOUT
THE PILOT USES HAND CONTROLS AND FOOT PEDALS TO STEER THE AIRPLANE. THE CONTROLS MOVE FLAPS ON THE PLANE'S WINGS AND TAIL.
WHEN THE PILOT MOVES THE CONTROL COLUMN LEFT OR RIGHT, THE FLAP (AILERON) ON ONE WING IS RAISED AND THE FLAP ON THE OPPOSITE WING IS LOWERED. THIS CAUSES THE PLANE TO ROLL.
TO CLIMB OR DIVE, THE PILOT PULLS OR PUSHES THE CONTROL COLUMN. THIS RAISES OR LOWERS THE FLAPS (ELEVATORS) LOCATED ON THE TAIL. WHEN PULLED, THE AIRPLANE GOES UP OR CLIMBS. WHEN PUSHED IT GOES DOWN OR DIVES.
WE CAN CARRY OVER 400 PASSENGERS.
I DON'T HAVE A TICKET!
PUSHING ON THE FOOT PEDALS TURNS THE RUDDER FLAP ON THE TAIL, CAUSING THE PLANE TO TURN LEFT OR RIGHT. TO TURN SMOOTHLY, THE PILOT ROLLS THE PLANE AT THE SAME TIME.
JET ENGINES SUCK AIR IN LIKE A VACUUM AND MIX IT WITH FUEL. THE BURNING MIXTURE IS BLASTED OUT THE REAR OF THE ENGINE, "PUSHING" THE AIRPLANE THROUGH THE AIR.
AIR IN
PUSHES THE PLANE
TURBOJET ENGINES
A GLIDER HAS NO ENGINE. THE LONG WINGS PRODUCE A HIGH LIFT AT VERY SLOW SPEEDS.
I'M THE SUPERSONIC TRANSPORT.
X-1 WAS FIRST PLANE LY FASTER N THE SPEED SOUND.
I'M A PRIVATE LIGHT PLANE.
PISTON ENGINES ARE THE SAME AS THOSE IN AUTOMOBILES. THEY ARE ATTACHED TO PROPELLERS WHICH "PULL" THE AIRPLANE THROUGH THE AIR.
SOME JETS HAVE ENGINES ON THEIR TAIL.
REAR ENGINE EXHAUST
HOW TO FLY
I'M A SMALL CORPORATE JET.
I'M THE WRIGHT BROTHERS FIRST AIRPLANE (1903). MY PROPELLERS WERE ON THE BACK.
E SLOWER VING AIR NEATH THE G PUSHES E WING WARD, REATING LIFT."
BLUE IS AIR FLOW
CLIMBING
DIVING
ROLLING

LASERS

A laser is a device that intensifies or increases light. It produces a thin beam of light, stronger than sunlight, that can burn a hole through diamond or steel.

The first operational laser was built in 1960.

See if you can find all the things you did or didn't know about lasers in this picture. Don't forget to look for the following fun things, too.

- ☐ Apple
- ☐ Book
- ☐ Cheerleader
- ☐ Chicken
- ☐ Clock
- ☐ Drum
- ☐ Electrodes (2)
- ☐ Envelope
- ☐ Fish tank
- ☐ Flamingo
- ☐ Football
- ☐ Frog
- ☐ Globe
- ☐ Hot dog
- ☐ Little Red Riding Hood
- ☐ Mouse
- ☐ Necktie
- ☐ Orangutan
- ☐ Painted egg
- ☐ Paper airplane
- ☐ Parrot
- ☐ Roller skates
- ☐ Stapler
- ☐ Stethoscope
- ☐ Straw
- ☐ Thermometer
- ☐ Umbrella
- ☐ Vase

Name two types of lasers.
What are some of the uses of laser beams?

IN ORDINARY LIGHT, SUCH AS THAT FROM A LIGHT BULB, THE LIGHT WAVES GO OUT IN MANY DIFFERENT DIRECTIONS.

IN A LASER BEAM, THE LIGHT WAVES ALL HAVE THE SAME LENGTH AND TRAVEL IN THE SAME DIRECTION, PRODUCING A NARROW, INTENSE BEAM OF LIGHT.

HOORAY FOR LASERS.

I DON'T NEED A GAS MASK.

IS THIS THE GYM CLASS?

I'M IN THE MARCHING BAND.

I WANT ONE.

LASERS COME IN MANY SHAPES AND SIZES.

SOLID-STATE LASERS USE A MATERIAL SUCH AS RUBY, EMERALD, OR GLASS CRYSTAL TO PRODUCE BURSTS OF LIGHT.

GAS LASERS ARE MADE IN A GAS-FILLED TUBE AND PRODUCE A CONTINUOUS BEAM OF LIGHT.

GAS LASER

GAS-FILLED TUBE

MIRROR

ELECTRODE

ELECTRODE

SEMI-SILVERED MIRROR

I'LL PUNCH YOU IN THE NOSE.

I DON'T HAVE A NOSE.

THE MATERIAL USED TO CREATE LASER LIGHT IS CALLED A "MEDIUM." IT MAY BE SOLID, GAS, OR EVEN LIQUID.

TO PRODUCE A BEAM OF LASER LIGHT, ENERGY FROM A POWER SOURCE, SUCH AS AN ELECTRIC CURRENT, EXCITES THE ATOMS OF THE MEDIUM CAUSING THEM TO STRIKE EACH OTHER AND GIVE OFF LIGHT.

MIRRORS ARE USED WITHIN THE LASER TUBE TO INCREASE THE LIGHT-PRODUCING ATOM.

THIS IS WHAT THE WORD LASER STANDS FOR.
LIGHT AMPLIFICATION BY STIMULATED EMISSION OF RADIATION.
POLLY WANTS A LASER.
I'M LATE!
SOME LASERS PRODUCE INVISIBLE, INFRA-RED LIGHT BEAMS.
IT'S THE INVISIBLE STUDENT!
I SAW HIM!
I SAW HER!
TRICK OR TREAT
AFTER SCHOOL, I'M GOING TO MY GRANDMOTHER'S HOUSE.
I THOUGHT WE WERE GOING TO PLAY HIDE AND SEEK!
WE'RE HERE FOR SHOW AND TELL.
THAT'S A BRIGHT IDEA.
CAN A LASER DO MY HOMEWORK?
...AND MANY OTHERS.
...AND VIDEO DISCS.
...AND COMPACT DISCS.
...AND WEAPONS GUIDANCE SYSTEMS.
...AND TELEPHONE NETWORKS.
...AND DRILLING.
DON'T FORGET WELDING.
RS HAVE MANY
CTICAL USES,
LUDING
GICAL
CEDURES.
NO,
A
URGEON.
R-R-RING!
THE ENERGY OF A LASER BEAM CONCENTRATED ON A SMALL AREA MAY REACH TEMPERATURES HIGHER THAN 10,000 DEGREES.
WOW! THAT'S HOT!!
I DETECT HEAT!
DR. FRANKENSTEIN USED A LASER TO MAKE ME.
I WISH THIS WAS MINE!
I'M A STURGEON.
IT'S TOO HOT FOR ME!
?
NEXT PAGE.
LOGRAMS
E MADE
NG LASER
LIGHTS.
A HOLOGRAM LET'S YOU SEE A THREE-DIMENSIONAL VIEW OF A PICTURE OF AN OBJECT.
I SAW A LASER LIGHT SHOW AT THE ROCK CONCERT.
ROCKS GIVE CONCERTS?
I DIDN'T KNOW THAT!
I KNOW IT NOW!

SPORTS

Search and find lots of interesting facts about:

- **Soccer**
- **Swimming**
- **Basketball**
- **Gymnastics**
- **Baseball**
- **Bowling**
- **Football**
- **Ice Hockey**
- **Tennis**
- **Martial Arts**
- **Track and Field**

SOCCER
Soccer is the most popular participant sport in the world.
Soccer's history can be traced back over 2,000 years. Its action is almost nonstop as two teams move continuously up and down the field, each trying to kick or head the ball into the goal.
See if you can find all the things you did or didn't know about soccer in this picture. Don't forget to look for the following fun things, too.
☐ Artist
☐ Axe
☐ Banana peels (2)
☐ Basketball
☐ Bigfoot
☐ Bone
☐ Broom
☐ Camel
☐ Chef's hat
☐ Clock
☐ Cow
☐ Crown
☐ Firecracker
☐ Football
☐ Graduate
☐ Heart
☐ Hockey stick
☐ Jack-o'-lantern
☐ Juggler
☐ Jump rope
☐ Moose head
☐ Pinocchio
☐ Scarecrow
☐ Scuba diver
☐ Seal
☐ Stars (3)
☐ Trumpet
☐ Turtle
☐ Unicorn
☐ Witch
What is the World Cup?
How many players are on the soccer field at one time?
SOCCER FIELDS ARE BETWEEN 100-130 YARDS LONG AND 70-100 YARDS WIDE.
KNOCK-TV
AT EITHER END ARE THE GOALS AND RECTANGULAR GOAL AREAS.
THE BALL IS USUALLY MADE OF LEATHER AND IS ABOUT 27-28 INCHES AROUND. KIDS USE A SMALLER BALL.
IT WEIGHS LESS THAN ONE POUND.
EACH TEAM FIELDS 11 PLAYERS.
ADULTS PLAY TWO 45-MINUTE HALVES.
THE CLOCK RUNS CONTINUOUSLY EVEN WHEN A GOAL IS SCORED OR THE BALL GOES OUT-OF-BOUNDS.
12 YEARS AND UNDER LEAGUES PLAY TWO 30-MINUTE HALVES.
WHAT TIME IS IT?
I'M LATE!
I THOUGHT THIS WAS A ROCK CONCERT!
GO TEAM!
THIS IS THE PLACE.
I'M PLAYING!
I DETECT THE TEAMS WARMING UP.
WE'VE ARRIVED!!
PLAYERS USE THEIR FOREHEADS FOR HEADING AND THEIR INSTEPS FOR LONG PASSES AND FOR SHOTS ON GOAL.
THE BALL TRAVELS FASTER WHEN KICKED WITH THE INSTEP.
I'M BIG FOOT!
I'M A STAR PLAYER!
EAT AT HOME!
A GAME SIMILAR TO SOCCER WAS PLAYED IN CHINA ABOUT 2400 YEARS AGO.
IN 1848, THE FIRST SET OF RULES WAS ESTABLISHED.
ONCE TAKEN OUT OF A GAME, A PLAYER CANNOT RETURN.
I'M TRYING OUT FOR THE TEAM!

THIS IS THE PLACE!
LOOK! NO HANDS.
IF A PENALTY OCCURS WITHIN THE PENALTY AREAS IN FRONT OF THE GOALS, A PENALTY KICK IS AWARDED.
GOAL LINE
TOUCH LINE
EACH GOAL HAS TWO WOODEN POSTS, 24 FEET APART AND JOINED AT THE TOP BY A CROSSBAR.
A NET IS ATTACHED WHICH STOPS THE BALL WHEN A GOAL IS SCORED.
GOAL AREA
PENALTY AREA
PENALTY SPOT
ONLY THE GOALKEEPERS INSIDE THE GOAL AREA ARE ALLOWED TO TOUCH THE BALL WITH THEIR HANDS.
ES ALONG SIDE ARE ALLED CH LINES.
A MEMBER OF THE OFFENSE GETS A KICK FROM ONLY 12 YARDS IN FRONT OF THE GOAL.
ONLY A GOALIE CAN BLOCK A PENALTY KICK.
OTHER PLAYERS CAN KICK THE BALL WITH THEIR FEET OR HIT IT WITH THEIR HEADS AND BODIES.
KEEP OFF THE GRASS
CENTER CIRCLE
A REFEREE AND TWO LINESMEN CONTROL THE GAME.
DRIBBLING IS MOVING THE BALL WITH CONTROL USING THE FEET.
A FORWARD PLAYER TAKES SHOTS AND SCORES GOALS.
A FULLBACK IS A DEFENSIVE PLAYER WHO TRIES TO KEEP THE OTHER TEAM FROM SCORING.
DING IS USING HEAD TO TRAP MOVE THE BALL.
A HALFBACK IS A MIDFIELD PLAYER WHO COVERS OFFENSE AND DEFENSE.
A SWEEPER IS A FULLBACK CLOSE TO THE GOAL WHO HELPS OTHER DEFENDERS.
A WING IS ANOTHER NAME FOR A LEFT OR RIGHT FORWARD.
A SAVE IS WHEN THE GOALIE CATCHES OR BLOCKS A BALL TO PREVENT A SCORE.
LET THE GAME BEGIN!
THERE'S THE NET... WHERE'S THE WATER?
TRAPPING IS USING THE BODY TO STOP AND CONTROL A BALL IN THE AIR.
Z-Z-Z!
PELÉ OF BRAZIL SCORED 1281 GOALS IN HIS CAREER.
BODY
THE WORLD CUP IS THE WORLD CHAMPIONSHIP SOCCER TOURNAMENT, HELD EVERY FOUR YEARS.
BRAZIL, ITALY, AND GERMANY HAVE EACH WON THREE WORLD CUPS.
I'M A GRADE "A" PLAYER!
HI, MOM!
GERD MÜLLER OF WEST GERMANY SCORED 14 CAREER WORLD CUP GOALS.

SWIMMING

On a hot summer day, is there anything more refreshing than swimming in a pool, lake, pond, ocean, or river? Swimming is one of the most popular forms of recreation, a wonderful exercise for keeping fit, and an exciting international sport.

See if you can find all the things you did or didn't know about swimming in this picture. Don't forget to look for the following fun things, too.

- ☐ Backpack
- ☐ Birdbath
- ☐ Book
- ☐ Cactus
- ☐ Divers (2)
- ☐ Fisherman
- ☐ Flamingo
- ☐ Flying bat
- ☐ Football helmet
- ☐ Heart
- ☐ Lost sock
- ☐ Mark Spitz
- ☐ Mermaids (2)
- ☐ Monkey
- ☐ Oil can
- ☐ Owl
- ☐ Pencil
- ☐ Robot
- ☐ Roller skater
- ☐ Rubber ducky
- ☐ Sailboat
- ☐ Sandcastle
- ☐ Shark fin
- ☐ Skunk
- ☐ Submarine
- ☐ Superhero
- ☐ Surfer
- ☐ Tarzan

Name the American swimmer who won nine gold medals in the 1968 and 1972 Olympics?
Who was the first woman to swim the English Channel?

I BROUGHT MY OWN SOAP!
NEAR EACH END OF THE POOL, A LINE OF FLAGS IS HUNG OVER THE WATER TO WARN BACK-STROKE SWIMMERS THAT THEY ARE APPROACHING THE END OF THE LANE.
I CAN'T SWIM!
WALL TARGETS AT THE END OF EACH LANE AND MARKERS AT THE BOTTOM OF THE POOL GUIDE THE SWIMMERS.
TO START THE RACE, SWIMMERS DIVE OFF A RAISED PLATFORM.
IN BACKSTROKE EVENTS THEY START IN THE WATER.
ECTRONIC G AND NG SYSTEM MINES ORDER SH AND SWIMMER'S E.
FALSE START LINE
AN ILLEGAL STROKE OR TURN DISQUALIFIES A SWIMMER.
S CALLED LINES THE GTH OF POOL. HELP P THE R CALM MARK NE DARIES.
SWIM MEETS ARE HELD IN LONG-COURSE POOLS, 50 METERS LONG AND SHORT-COURSE POOLS, 22.885 METERS LONG.
AWL AND CKSTROKE IMMERS USE FLIP TURN.
WATER MUST BE AT LEAST FOUR FEET DEEP AND 78° F.
LEG KICKS COMBINED WITH ARM MOVEMENTS ARE CALLED STROKES.
THERE ARE FOUR BASIC TYPES OF KICKS: FLUTTER, BREASTSTROKE, DOLPHIN, AND THE SCISSORS KICK.
BASIC STROKES:
FRONT CRAWL
BACKSTROKE
BUTTERFLY
BREASTSTROKE
NOW I KNOW IT!
OTHER STROKES INCLUDE: SIDESTROKE, DOG PADDLE, AND ELEMENTARY BACKSTROKE.
THE CRAWL IS THE FASTEST AND MOST POPULAR STROKE.
I DO THE DOG PADDLE BEST.

INVENTOR OF BASKETBALL
#1
DR. JAMES A. NAISMITH
THE FIRST BASKETBALL GAME WAS PLAYED IN THE YMCA BASEMENT GYM IN SPRINGFIELD, MASSACHUSETTS.
TWO HALF-BUSHEL PEACH BASKETS SERVED AS GOALS.
THEY USED A SOCCER BALL.
THE FIRST BASKETBALLS WERE MADE OF LEATHER AND HAD LACES (1894).
TODAY'S BALL IS MOLDED OF RUBBER OR PLASTIC AND INFLATED WITH AIR, AND IS ABOUT 30 INCHES IN CIRCUMFERENCE.
IN 1936, UNITED WON THE GOLD M AWARDE BASKET IN THE OLYMPI
THEY DEFEATED CANADA 19-8. THE GAME WAS PLAYED OUTDOORS IN THE RAIN!
I WONDER IF HE WAS TALL?
HE WAS A PHYSICAL-EDUCATION TEACHER AND WANTED A GAME THAT COULD BE PLAYED INDOORS DURING THE WINTER.
THE FIRST OFFICIAL GAME WAS PLAYED ON MARCH 20, 1897.
YALE BEAT PENNSYLVANIA, 35-10.
I LOVE WATCHING "ROUND-BALL!"
HI!
SCO
ALL LINES ARE 2 INCHES WIDE
WHERE'S THE BALL?
OOPS!
SMILE! YOU'RE ON TV.
WILT CHAMBERLAI WAS THE FIRST A ONLY PLAYER TO SCORE 100 POINT IN AN NBA GAME
BACKBOARD
HOW ABOUT USING ME?
26
3 POINT LINE (COLLEGIATE)
13
RESTR CIRCL
FREE THROW LINE
15 FEET
3 POINT LINE (PROFESSIONAL)
IF YOU COMMIT SIX FOU IN AN N GAME Y ARE DISQUAL
THE FIRST PROFESSIONAL BASKETBALL GAME WAS PLAYED IN 1896 IN TRENTON, NEW JERSEY.
FREE THROW LANE
THROW THE BALL TO ME!
ME, TOO!
16
87
THE LI IS FIVE FOULS COLLEG
GO TEAM
REAL #1
IN 1992, PROS CO IN THE OLYMPI FOR THE FIRST
FIELD GOALS ARE EITHER 2 OR 3 POINTS DEPENDING ON THE DISTANCE FROM WHERE THEY ARE SHOT.
FOUL SHOTS, OR FREE THROWS, COUNT AS 1 POINT.
DRIBBLE - TO BOUNCE THE BALL ON THE FLOOR BY PUSHING IT WITH ONE HAND.
REBOUND - TO GRAB THE BALL OFF THE BASKET RIM OR BACKBOARD AFTER AN UNSUCCESSFUL SHOT.
A FOUL OCCURS WHEN ONE PLAYER PUSHES, HOLDS, OR CHARGES INTO ANOTHER.
THE FOULED PLAYER IS EITHER AWARDED FREE THROWS OR POSSESSION OF THE BALL.
COLLEGE AND PROFESSIONAL COURTS ARE 94 FEET LONG AND 50 FEET WIDE.

BASKETBALL

Basketball is played in over 130 countries throughout the world. To play, all you need is a ball, a basket, and a level surface. Basketball can be played indoors or out, alone or with others, night or day, 365 days a year!

See if you can find all the things you did or didn't know about basketball in this picture. Don't forget to look for the following fun things, too.

- ☐ Ballerina
- ☐ Balloons (5)
- ☐ Banana peel
- ☐ Bowling ball
- ☐ Boxing glove
- ☐ Bucket
- ☐ Bushel basket
- ☐ Cane
- ☐ Clock
- ☐ Crown
- ☐ Fish
- ☐ Football
- ☐ Graduate
- ☐ Ice skate
- ☐ Ice-cream cone
- ☐ Kite
- ☐ Lost shoe
- ☐ Mermaid
- ☐ Monkey
- ☐ Mouse
- ☐ Pencil
- ☐ Piggy bank
- ☐ Scarecrow
- ☐ Skateboard
- ☐ Soccer ball
- ☐ Top hat
- ☐ Turtle

Name the NBA career scoring leader.

TIMER

PROFESSIONAL TEAMS PLAY FOUR 12 MINUTE QUARTERS, OR 48 MINUTES.

THE MOST POINTS IN NBA HISTORY WERE SCORED BY KAREEM ABDUL-JABBAR–38,387!

I'M NOT ON THE TEAM.

I'M IN THE WRONG GAME.

I SCORED 3 POINTS ALL SEASON.

BLOCK THE SHOT!

BASKETS ARE TEN FEET ABOVE THE GROUND AND 18 INCHES IN DIAMETER.

THE BACKBOARDS ARE 72 INCHES WIDE AND 48 INCHES HIGH.

THE NET SLOWS THE BALL DOWN AS IT GOES THROUGH THE BASKET.

CENTER LINE

I'M LOST.

EARVIN "MAGIC" JOHNSON WAS A LONG-TIME ASSIST LEADER.

THE FOUL LINE IS 15 FEET FROM THE BACKBOARD.

?

WILT CHAMBERLAIN HAD 55 REBOUNDS IN ONE GAME!

PRO PLAYERS MUST SHOOT THE BALL WITHIN 24 SECONDS – COLLEGE PLAYERS WITHIN 45 SECONDS.

IN 1977, TED ST MARTIN MADE 2,036 CONSECUTIVE FOUL SHOTS!

MICHAEL JORDAN IS THE WORLD'S MOST EXCITING PLAYER TODAY.

WILT CHAMBERLAIN PLAYED 1,045 GAMES (HIS ENTIRE CAREER) WITHOUT FOULING OUT!

I SURE DID.

COULD SHE SLAM-DUNK?

PEARL MOORE SCORED 4,061 POINTS FOR FRANCIS MARION COLLEGE – THE MOST BY A WOMAN IN A COLLEGE CAREER!

I DIDN'T KNOW THAT!

I KNOW IT NOW!

GYMNASTICS

In gymnastics, acrobatic exercises are performed on various pieces of equipment. Gymnastics helps develop balance, agility, and strength. During the 1970's Olympics, the emergence of two superstars — Olga Korbut and Nadia Comaneci — gave gymnastics worldwide popularity.

See if you can find all the things you did or didn't know about gymnastics in this picture. Don't forget to look for the following fun things, too.

- ☐ Banana peel
- ☐ Bear
- ☐ Broom
- ☐ Crown
- ☐ Crutch
- ☐ Doctor
- ☐ Duck
- ☐ Elephant
- ☐ Exercise bike
- ☐ Football
- ☐ Jogger
- ☐ Juggler
- ☐ Kangaroo
- ☐ Mail carrier
- ☐ Pillow
- ☐ Scarecrow
- ☐ Shovel
- ☐ Snowman
- ☐ Star
- ☐ Telescope
- ☐ Top hat
- ☐ TV camera
- ☐ Unicorn
- ☐ Water skier
- ☐ Wooden spoon

Who first achieved a perfect mark of 10 in the Olympics?
What are the six events men compete in?

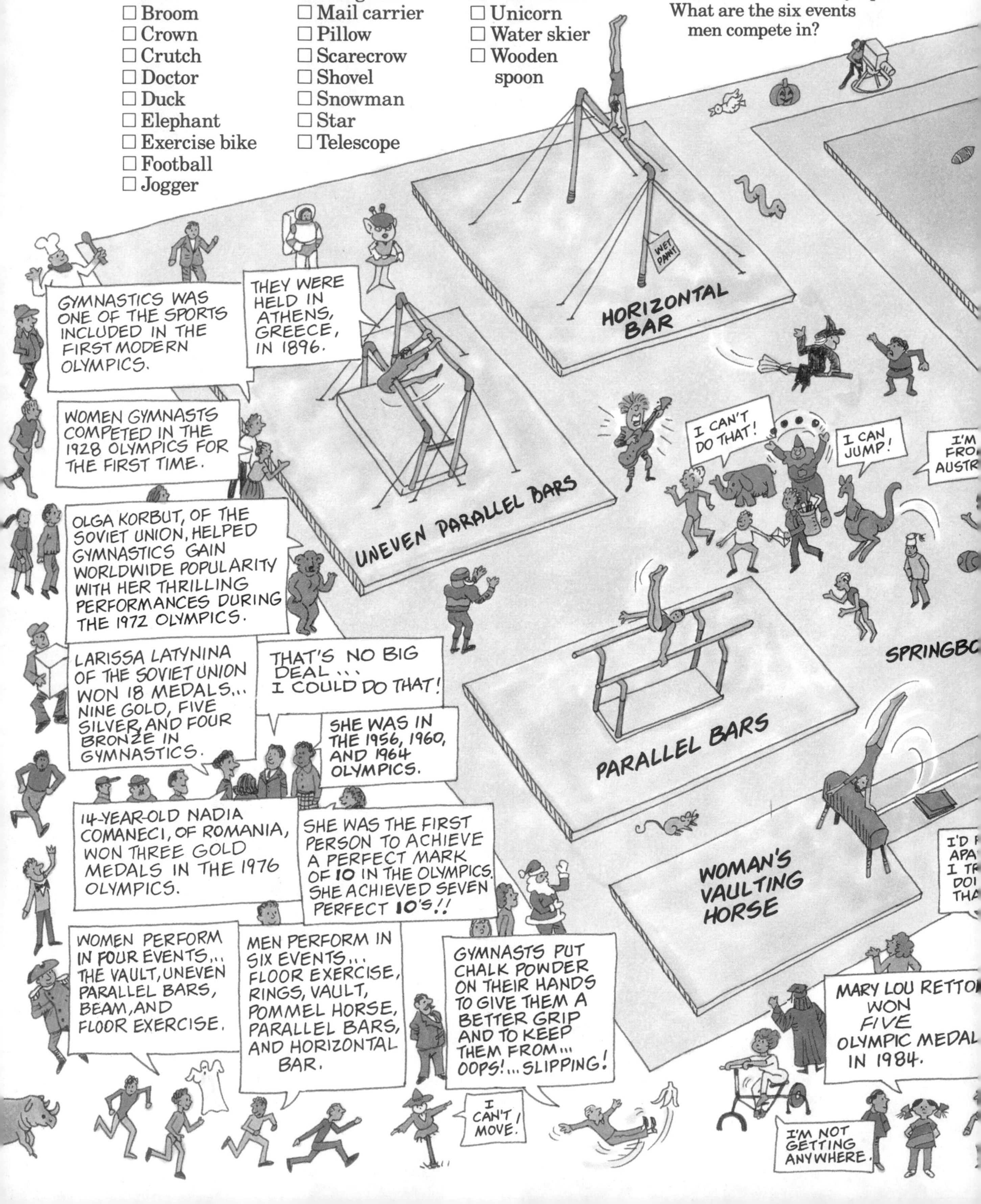

WET PAINT
HORIZONTAL BAR
GYMNASTICS WAS ONE OF THE SPORTS INCLUDED IN THE FIRST MODERN OLYMPICS.
THEY WERE HELD IN ATHENS, GREECE, IN 1896.
WOMEN GYMNASTS COMPETED IN THE 1928 OLYMPICS FOR THE FIRST TIME.
UNEVEN PARALLEL BARS
I CAN'T DO THAT!
I CAN JUMP!
I'M FRO
AUSTR
OLGA KORBUT, OF THE SOVIET UNION, HELPED GYMNASTICS GAIN WORLDWIDE POPULARITY WITH HER THRILLING PERFORMANCES DURING THE 1972 OLYMPICS.
SPRINGBO
LARISSA LATYNINA OF THE SOVIET UNION WON 18 MEDALS... NINE GOLD, FIVE SILVER, AND FOUR BRONZE IN GYMNASTICS.
THAT'S NO BIG DEAL... I COULD DO THAT!
SHE WAS IN THE 1956, 1960, AND 1964 OLYMPICS.
PARALLEL BARS
14-YEAR-OLD NADIA COMANECI, OF ROMANIA, WON THREE GOLD MEDALS IN THE 1976 OLYMPICS.
SHE WAS THE FIRST PERSON TO ACHIEVE A PERFECT MARK OF 10 IN THE OLYMPICS. SHE ACHIEVED SEVEN PERFECT 10'S!!
WOMAN'S VAULTING HORSE
I'D
APA
I TR
DOI
THA
WOMEN PERFORM IN FOUR EVENTS... THE VAULT, UNEVEN PARALLEL BARS, BEAM, AND FLOOR EXERCISE.
MEN PERFORM IN SIX EVENTS... FLOOR EXERCISE, RINGS, VAULT, POMMEL HORSE, PARALLEL BARS, AND HORIZONTAL BAR.
GYMNASTS PUT CHALK POWDER ON THEIR HANDS TO GIVE THEM A BETTER GRIP AND TO KEEP THEM FROM... OOPS!... SLIPPING!
MARY LOU RETTO WON FIVE OLYMPIC MEDAL IN 1984.
I CAN'T MOVE!
I'M NOT GETTING ANYWHERE.

BALANCE BEAM
THREE FEET HIGH.
GYMNAST WALKS,
NS, LEAPS, JUMPS,
D BALANCES ON
EAM THAT IS
R INCHES WIDE.
WHERE'S SANTA?
MEN MUST HOLD THEIR BALANCE ON THE BARS AND RINGS FOR AT LEAST TWO SECONDS.
THERE GOES MY COUSIN!
BALANCE BEAM
POMMEL HORSE
RINGS
RINGS ARE ALMOST NINE FEET ABOVE THE GROUND.
I FELL!
WHERE'S THE ICE?
MEN'S VAULTING HORSE
FLOOR EXERCISE
T USED HERE
A SQUARE
VERING 39¼
EET OF
URFACE.
SPRINGBOARD
RUN!
THEY ARE ALL OLYMPIC STARS!
HOW DID I GET HERE?
FLOOR EXERCISE IS PERFORMED TO MUSIC. IT IS A MIXTURE OF DANCE, BALANCE, AND ACROBATICS.
INDIVIDUAL AND OVERALL MEDALS ARE AWARDED.
IN RHYTHMIC GYMNASTICS, THE GYMNAST MUST USE DANCE STEPS TAKEN FROM BALLET!
WHERE'S THE SNOWMAN?
THE OTHER MARKS ARE AVERAGED.
THE HIGHEST AND LOWEST MARKS DON'T COUNT.
A PANEL OF SIX JUDGES WATCHES AND MARKS EACH PERFORMANCE.
WHERE'S MY BONE?
DON'T ASK ME!
THE POMMEL HORSE IS ALSO KNOWN AS THE SIDE HORSE.
IT HAS TWO WOODEN HANDLES ON TOP CALLED POMMELS. THEY ARE ABOUT 50 INCHES FROM THE FLOOR.
NASTICS
DEVELOPED
ERMANY IN
EARLY 1800'S.
GYMNASTS NEED BALANCE, STRENGTH, AND FLEXIBILITY.
I'M FROM AUSTRALIA.
THE HORSE IS 64 INCHES LONG AND 14 INCHES WIDE.
WHERE'S THE WATER?

BASEBALL

Baseball, known as America's favorite pastime, is a game that most people have either watched or played. Developed from the English game of "rounders" in the 1700s, baseball is now an organized professional game with both major league and minor league teams. With thousands of games played each season—from Little League to the Majors—cries of "take me out to the ball game" can easily be fulfilled.

See if you can find all the things you did or didn't know about baseball in this picture. Don't forget to look for the following fun things, too!

- ☐ Arrow
- ☐ Bee
- ☐ Bone
- ☐ Bowling ball
- ☐ Broadcaster
- ☐ Bunny
- ☐ Dracula
- ☐ Duck
- ☐ Feather
- ☐ Fish
- ☐ Football helmet
- ☐ Ghosts (2)
- ☐ Graduate
- ☐ Hot dog vendor
- ☐ Ice-cream cone
- ☐ Jack-o'-lantern
- ☐ Mouse
- ☐ Periscope
- ☐ Propeller
- ☐ Ruler
- ☐ Santa Claus
- ☐ Star
- ☐ Straw
- ☐ Telescope
- ☐ Turtle
- ☐ Umbrella
- ☐ Witch's hat
- ☐ Worm

Who is the father of organized baseball?

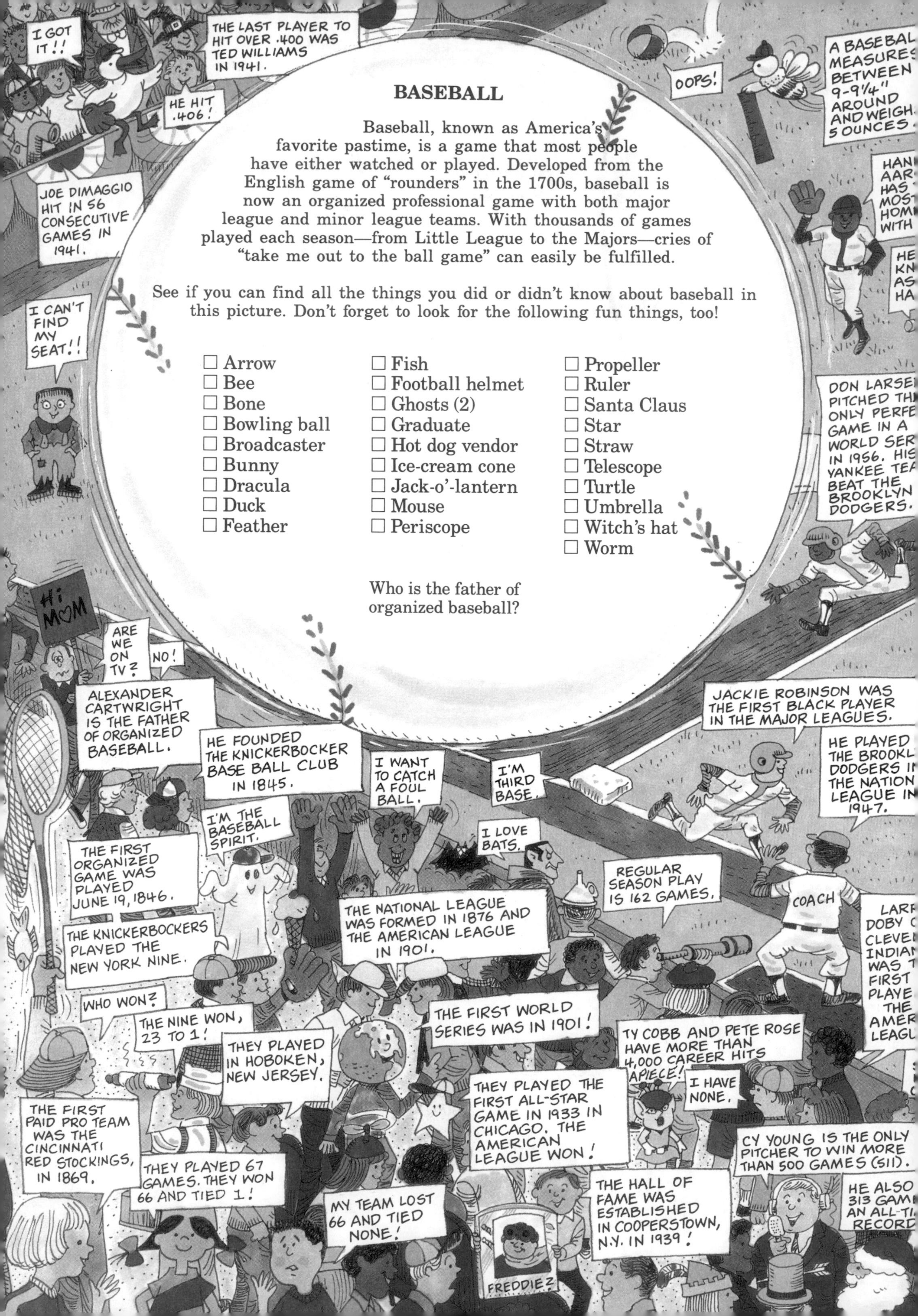

WHO'S ON FIRST?
IT'S 3 STRIKES AND YOU'RE OUT. THE STRIKE ZONE IS ANY PLACE OVER HOME PLATE BETWEEN THE BATTER'S ARMPITS AND KNEES!
I'M THE DESIGNATED BOOER.
I'M THE DESIGNATED HOT DOG EATER.
LET'S DO A WAVE.
THERE ARE 9 PLAYERS ON A NATIONAL LEAGUE TEAM AND 10 ON AN AMERICAN LEAGUE TEAM AS THEY HAVE A DESIGNATED HITTER.
I'M THE TEAM MASCOT.
IT TAKES 4 BALLS TO WALK. A BALL IS A PITCH OUT OF THE STRIKE ZONE.
BABE RUTH HAD THE MOST HOME RUNS IN A SEASON WITH 60 IN 1927. ROGER MARIS BROKE HIS RECORD IN 1961 WITH 61.
I FORGOT MY GLOVE.
I'M IN THE FROG LITTLE LEAGUE!
RICKY HENDERSON HAS STOLEN THE MOST BASES! I'M TRYING TO STEAL SECOND BASE.
KEEP OFF THE GRASS
WAY!
I'M LOST!
THE DISTANCE BETWEEN EACH BASE IS 90 FEET.
A BASEBALL HAS A CORK CENTER SURROUNDED WITH LAYERS OF RUBBER AND FOAM. TWO STRIPS OF WHITE COWHIDE ARE THE FINAL COVER.
THE PITCHER'S MOUND IS 18' 10" AROUND. PITCHERS MUST KEEP ONE FOOT ON A PIECE OF RUBBER IN THE MIDDLE OF THE MOUND WHEN THEY PITCH. THE RUBBER IS 60' 6" FROM HOME PLATE.
I'M FIRST BASE!
THERE ARE 2 COACHES' BOXES, AN ON DECK CIRCLE, AND BULL PENS FOR EACH TEAM'S PITCHERS TO WARM UP!
THE BAT CAN'T BE ANY LONGER THAN 42" AND NO THICKER THAN 2 3/4" AT ITS THICKEST PART.
KLUNK!
FOUL BALL!!
COACH
FOUL LINES MARK THE BOUNDARIES OF THE FIELD.
THE VISITING TEAM BATS FIRST.
EACH TEAM GETS 3 OUTS PER INNING AND 9 INNINGS ARE PLAYED.
THERE IS NO TIME LIMIT IN BASEBALL.
A LEFT-HANDED PITCHER.
WHAT'S A "SOUTHPAW"?
THE CATCHER'S BOX IS 5' LONG AND 3' 7" WIDE AND IS IN FOUL TERRITORY!
IF A BASE RUNNER IS STRUCK BY A BATTED BALL, HE IS AUTOMATICALLY OUT!
THE AMERICAN LEAGUE AND THE NATIONAL LEAGUE EACH HAVE 2 DIVISIONS – EAST AND WEST!
IF A BATTED BALL HITS A FOUL POLE, IT'S A HOME RUN!
#1

BOWLING

Bowling is one of the oldest and most popular indoor sports. The ancient Egyptians bowled on alleys similar to ours over 7,000 years ago. More Americans participate in bowling than any other sport — over 71,000,000 men, women, and children.

See if you can find all the things you did or didn't know about bowling in this picture. Don't forget to look for the following fun things, too.

- ☐ Arrow
- ☐ Balloon
- ☐ Basketball
- ☐ Birdhouse
- ☐ Bomb
- ☐ Bone
- ☐ Book
- ☐ Broom
- ☐ Cheese
- ☐ Cup
- ☐ Envelope
- ☐ Fish
- ☐ Flying bat
- ☐ Football
- ☐ Fork
- ☐ Ghost
- ☐ Gutter ball
- ☐ Hammer
- ☐ Hearts (5)
- ☐ Ice-cream cone
- ☐ Jack-o'-lantern
- ☐ Key
- ☐ Mermaid
- ☐ Mouse
- ☐ Pencil
- ☐ Pizza slice
- ☐ Stars (2)
- ☐ Strike
- ☐ Watermelon slice
- ☐ Witch
- ☐ Worm

How many strikes do you need to score a perfect game?
What are the pins made of?

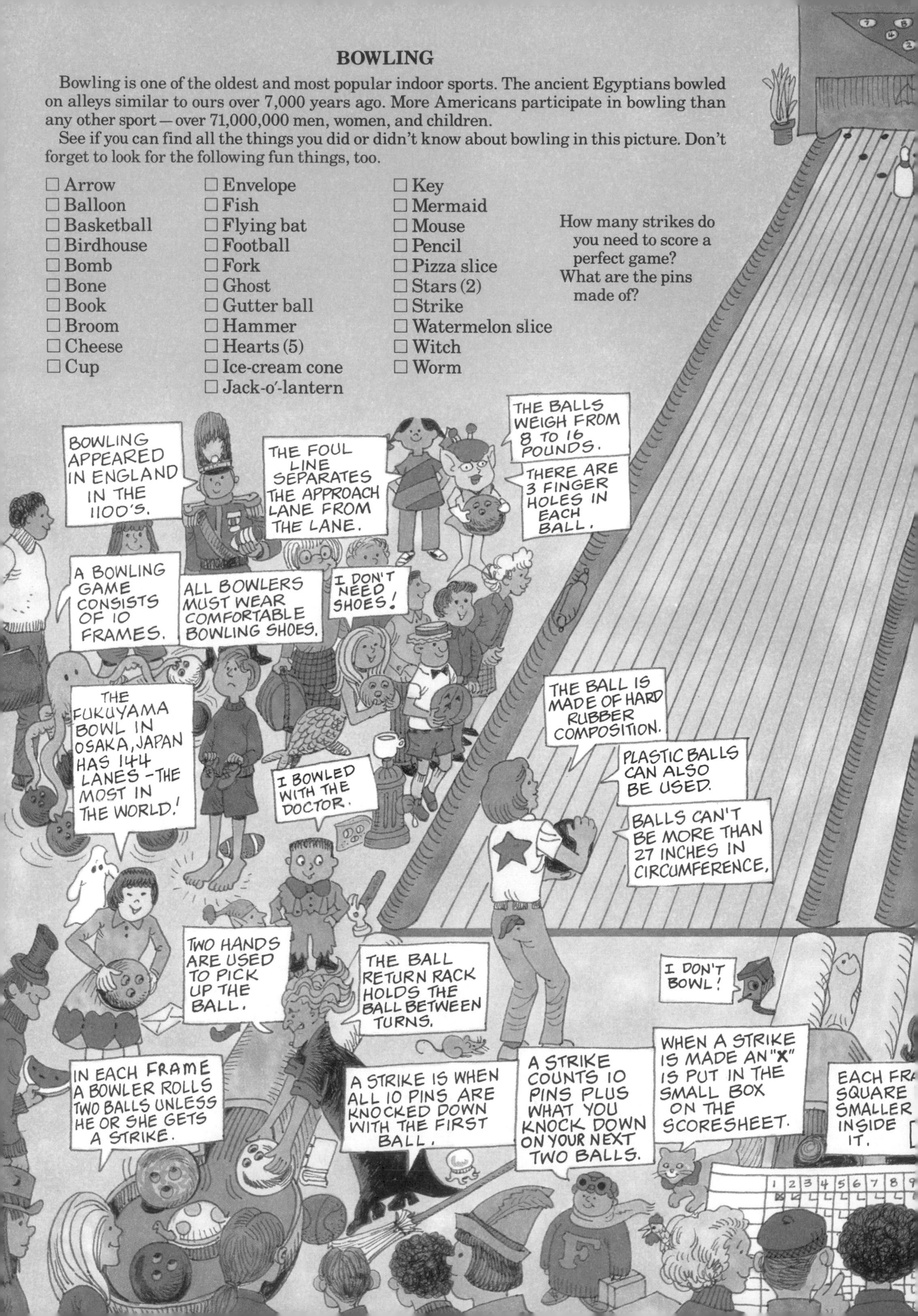

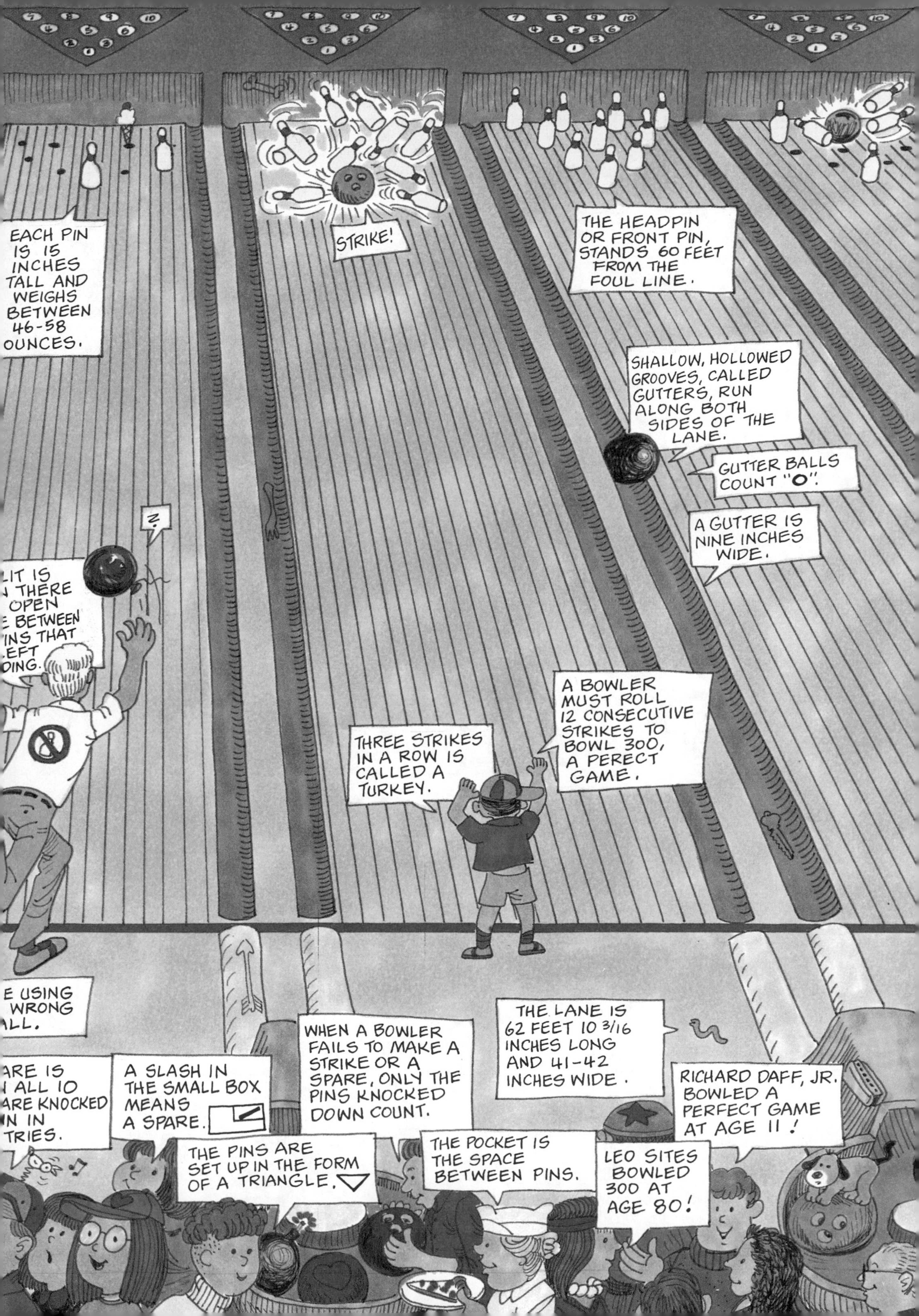

EACH PIN IS 15 INCHES TALL AND WEIGHS BETWEEN 46-58 OUNCES.
STRIKE!
THE HEADPIN OR FRONT PIN, STANDS 60 FEET FROM THE FOUL LINE.
SHALLOW, HOLLOWED GROOVES, CALLED GUTTERS, RUN ALONG BOTH SIDES OF THE LANE.
GUTTER BALLS COUNT "0".
A GUTTER IS NINE INCHES WIDE.
LIT IS N THERE OPEN E BETWEEN INS THAT EFT DING.
A BOWLER MUST ROLL 12 CONSECUTIVE STRIKES TO BOWL 300, A PERECT GAME.
THREE STRIKES IN A ROW IS CALLED A TURKEY.
E USING WRONG LL.
THE LANE IS 62 FEET 10 3/16 INCHES LONG AND 41-42 INCHES WIDE.
WHEN A BOWLER FAILS TO MAKE A STRIKE OR A SPARE, ONLY THE PINS KNOCKED DOWN COUNT.
ARE IS N ALL 10 ARE KNOCKED N IN TRIES.
A SLASH IN THE SMALL BOX MEANS A SPARE.
RICHARD DAFF, JR. BOWLED A PERFECT GAME AT AGE 11!
THE PINS ARE SET UP IN THE FORM OF A TRIANGLE.
THE POCKET IS THE SPACE BETWEEN PINS.
LEO SITES BOWLED 300 AT AGE 80!

FOOTBALL

On November 6, 1879, the universities of Rutgers and Princeton met in New Brunswick, New Jersey in the first college football game. Rutgers won 6-4.

The early games were a modified version of soccer and rugby. Football pioneers, such as Walter Camp, instituted 11 man teams, "downs" and yards to go, a smaller field, the line of scrimmage, and a new scoring system.

See if you can find all the things you did or didn't know about football in this picture. Don't forget to look for the following fun things, too.

- ☐ Air pump
- ☐ Arrow
- ☐ Birds (3)
- ☐ Blimp
- ☐ Bowling pin
- ☐ Candy cane
- ☐ Clipboard
- ☐ Fish
- ☐ Flying bat
- ☐ Ghost
- ☐ Hamburger
- ☐ Heart
- ☐ Horseshoe
- ☐ Hot dog
- ☐ Locker
- ☐ Lost sneaker
- ☐ Mask
- ☐ Mummy
- ☐ Pencil
- ☐ Snowman
- ☐ Straw
- ☐ Telescope
- ☐ Tinman
- ☐ Trophy
- ☐ Turtle
- ☐ Water bucket
- ☐ Whistle
- ☐ Worm

What is a punt?

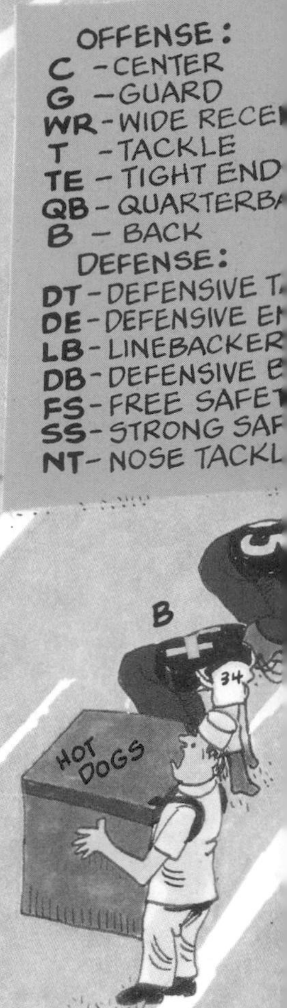

OFFENSE:
C - CENTER
G - GUARD
WR - WIDE RECE
T - TACKLE
TE - TIGHT END
QB - QUARTERBA
B - BACK
DEFENSE:
DT - DEFENSIVE T
DE - DEFENSIVE E
LB - LINEBACKER
DB - DEFENSIVE B
FS - FREE SAFET
SS - STRONG SAF
NT - NOSE TACKL

B
HOT DOGS
34

THE FIRST PRO GAME WAS PLAYED IN LATROBE, PA.

THERE ARE 28 TEAMS IN THE NFL. THE CHAMPIONSHIP IS CALLED THE SUPER BOWL.

THE FIRST SUPER BOWL WAS PLAYED IN 1967. THE GREEN BAY PACKERS BEAT THE KANSAS CITY CHIEFS, 35-10.

WR

THE NFL (NATIONAL FOOTBALL LEAGUE) WAS FORMED IN 1922.

GOAL POST

END ZONE

THE FIELD IS 100 YARDS LONG AND 160 FEET WIDE.
THE FIELD IS ALSO CALLED THE GRIDIRON.

50 YD. LINE

COACH

WHITE LINES, CALLED YARDLINES, RUN ACROSS THE FIELD EVERY FIVE YARDS.

HURRY UP WITH THAT BALL!

TWO ROWS OF SHORT WHITE LINES, CALLED HASH MARKS, SET ONE YARD APART RUN THE LENGTH OF THE FIELD. ALL PLAYS BEGIN WITH THE BALL ON OR BETWEEN THE HASH MARK

THE AIR-FILLED LEATHER BALL WEIGHS 14-15 OUNCES AND IS ABOUT 11 INCHES FROM POINT TO POINT.

END ZONE

GOAL POST

13

CARRYING OR PASSING THE BALL INTO THE OPPONENT'S END ZONE IS A TOUCHDOWN... GOOD FOR 6 POINTS. AN EXTRA POINT CAN THEN BE MADE BY KICKING THE BALL THROUGH THE GOAL POSTS.

OTHER POINTS:
FIELD GOAL - 3 POINTS. OCCURS WHEN THE BALL IS KICKED THROUGH THE OTHER TEAM'S GOAL POST.
SAFETY - 2 POINTS. OCCURS WHEN A PLAYER WITH THE BALL IS TACKLED IN HIS OWN END ZONE.

THE LACES PROVIDE A GOOD GRIP FOR PASSERS AND BALL CARRIERS.

F

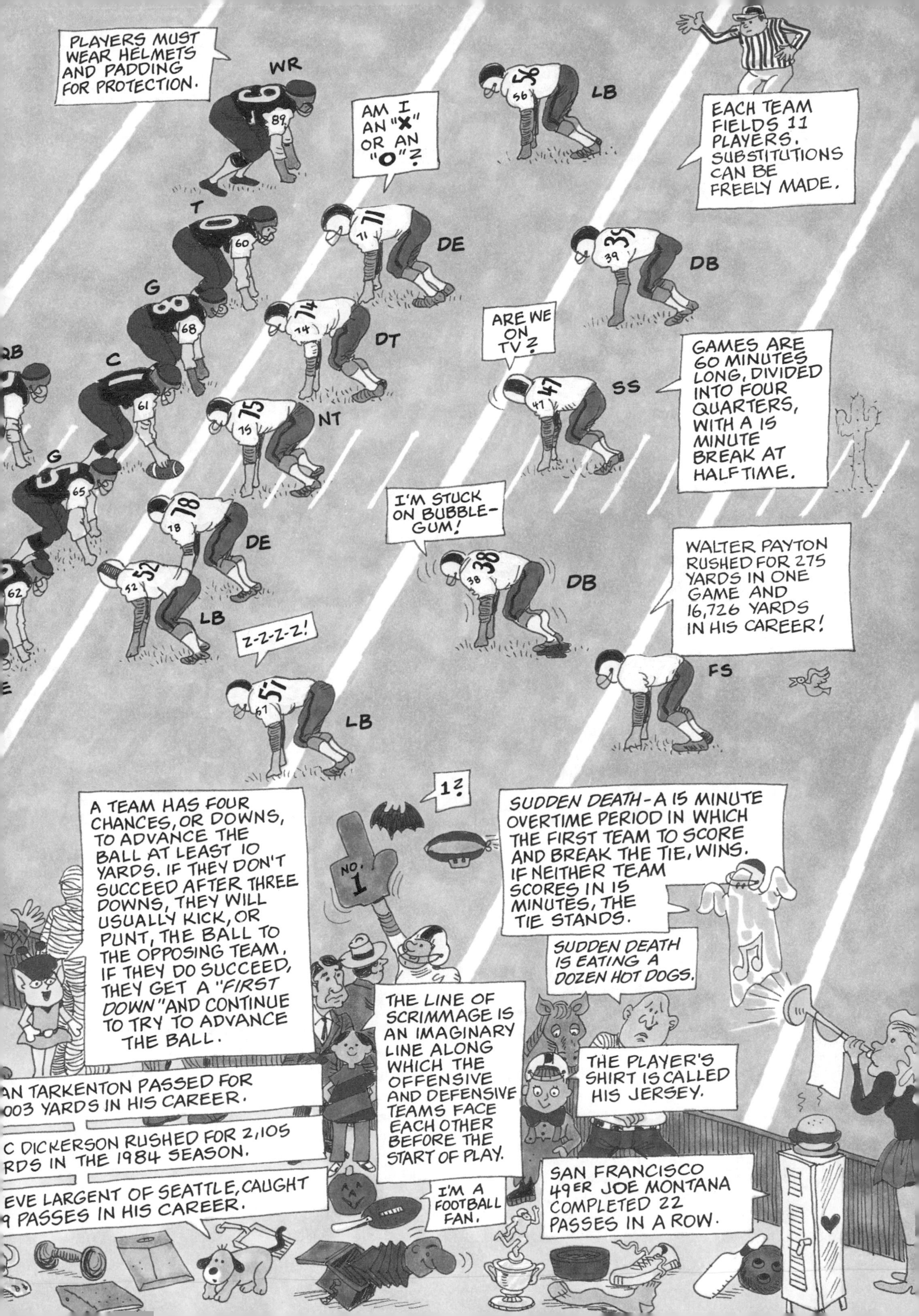

PLAYERS MUST WEAR HELMETS AND PADDING FOR PROTECTION.
WR
LB
AM I AN "X" OR AN "O"?
EACH TEAM FIELDS 11 PLAYERS. SUBSTITUTIONS CAN BE FREELY MADE.
T
DE
DB
G
DT
C
ARE WE ON TV?
SS
GAMES ARE 60 MINUTES LONG, DIVIDED INTO FOUR QUARTERS, WITH A 15 MINUTE BREAK AT HALFTIME.
NT
G
I'M STUCK ON BUBBLE-GUM!
DE
DB
WALTER PAYTON RUSHED FOR 275 YARDS IN ONE GAME AND 16,726 YARDS IN HIS CAREER!
LB
Z-Z-Z-Z!
FS
LB
1?
A TEAM HAS FOUR CHANCES, OR DOWNS, TO ADVANCE THE BALL AT LEAST 10 YARDS. IF THEY DON'T SUCCEED AFTER THREE DOWNS, THEY WILL USUALLY KICK, OR PUNT, THE BALL TO THE OPPOSING TEAM. IF THEY DO SUCCEED, THEY GET A "FIRST DOWN" AND CONTINUE TO TRY TO ADVANCE THE BALL.
NO. 1
SUDDEN DEATH - A 15 MINUTE OVERTIME PERIOD IN WHICH THE FIRST TEAM TO SCORE AND BREAK THE TIE, WINS. IF NEITHER TEAM SCORES IN 15 MINUTES, THE TIE STANDS.
SUDDEN DEATH IS EATING A DOZEN HOT DOGS.
THE LINE OF SCRIMMAGE IS AN IMAGINARY LINE ALONG WHICH THE OFFENSIVE AND DEFENSIVE TEAMS FACE EACH OTHER BEFORE THE START OF PLAY.
THE PLAYER'S SHIRT IS CALLED HIS JERSEY.
AN TARKENTON PASSED FOR 003 YARDS IN HIS CAREER.
C DICKERSON RUSHED FOR 2,105 RDS IN THE 1984 SEASON.
EVE LARGENT OF SEATTLE, CAUGHT 9 PASSES IN HIS CAREER.
I'M A FOOTBALL FAN.
SAN FRANCISCO 49ER JOE MONTANA COMPLETED 22 PASSES IN A ROW.

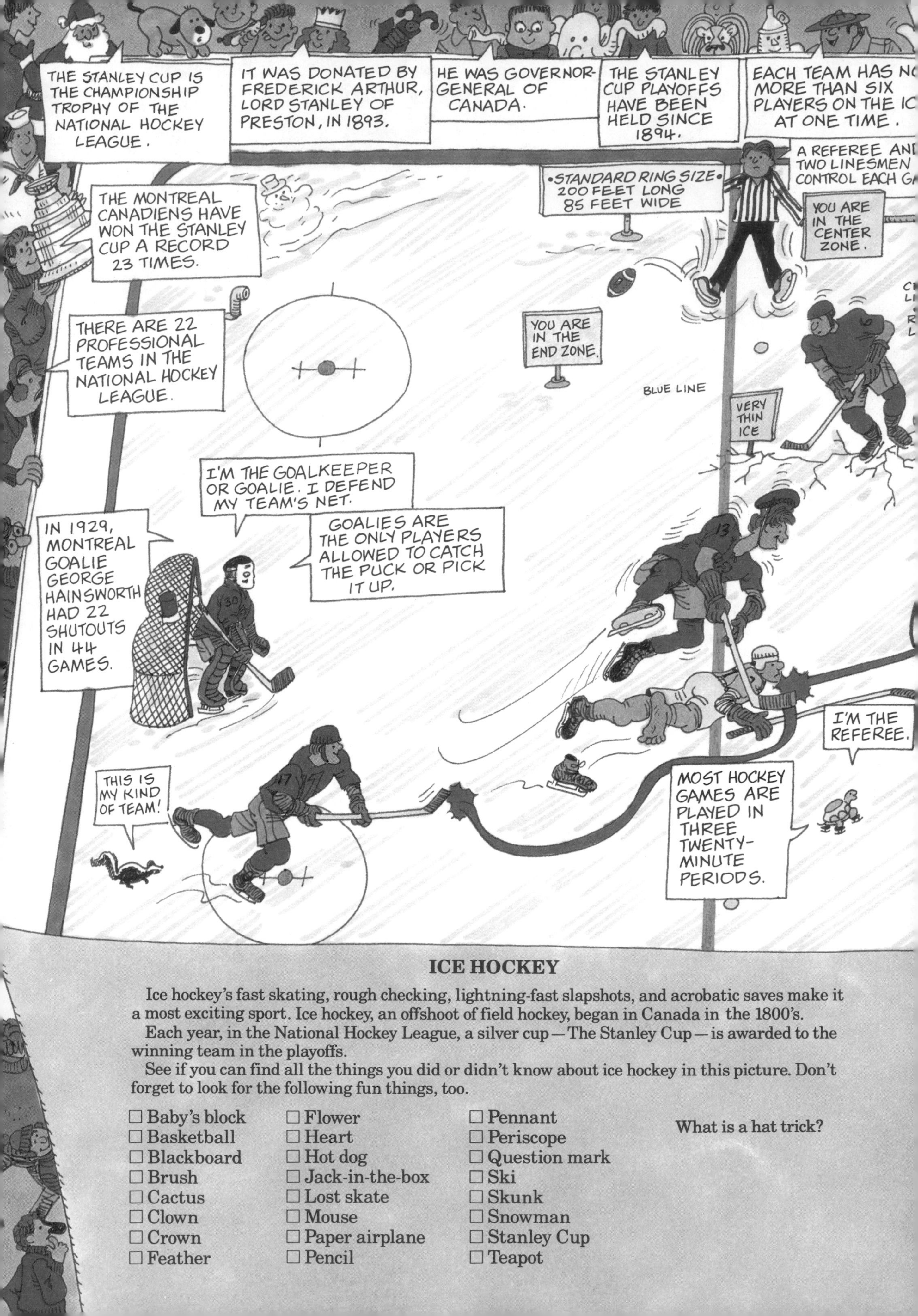

ICE HOCKEY

Ice hockey's fast skating, rough checking, lightning-fast slapshots, and acrobatic saves make it a most exciting sport. Ice hockey, an offshoot of field hockey, began in Canada in the 1800's.

Each year, in the National Hockey League, a silver cup — The Stanley Cup — is awarded to the winning team in the playoffs.

See if you can find all the things you did or didn't know about ice hockey in this picture. Don't forget to look for the following fun things, too.

- ☐ Baby's block
- ☐ Basketball
- ☐ Blackboard
- ☐ Brush
- ☐ Cactus
- ☐ Clown
- ☐ Crown
- ☐ Feather
- ☐ Flower
- ☐ Heart
- ☐ Hot dog
- ☐ Jack-in-the-box
- ☐ Lost skate
- ☐ Mouse
- ☐ Paper airplane
- ☐ Pencil
- ☐ Pennant
- ☐ Periscope
- ☐ Question mark
- ☐ Ski
- ☐ Skunk
- ☐ Snowman
- ☐ Stanley Cup
- ☐ Teapot

What is a hat trick?

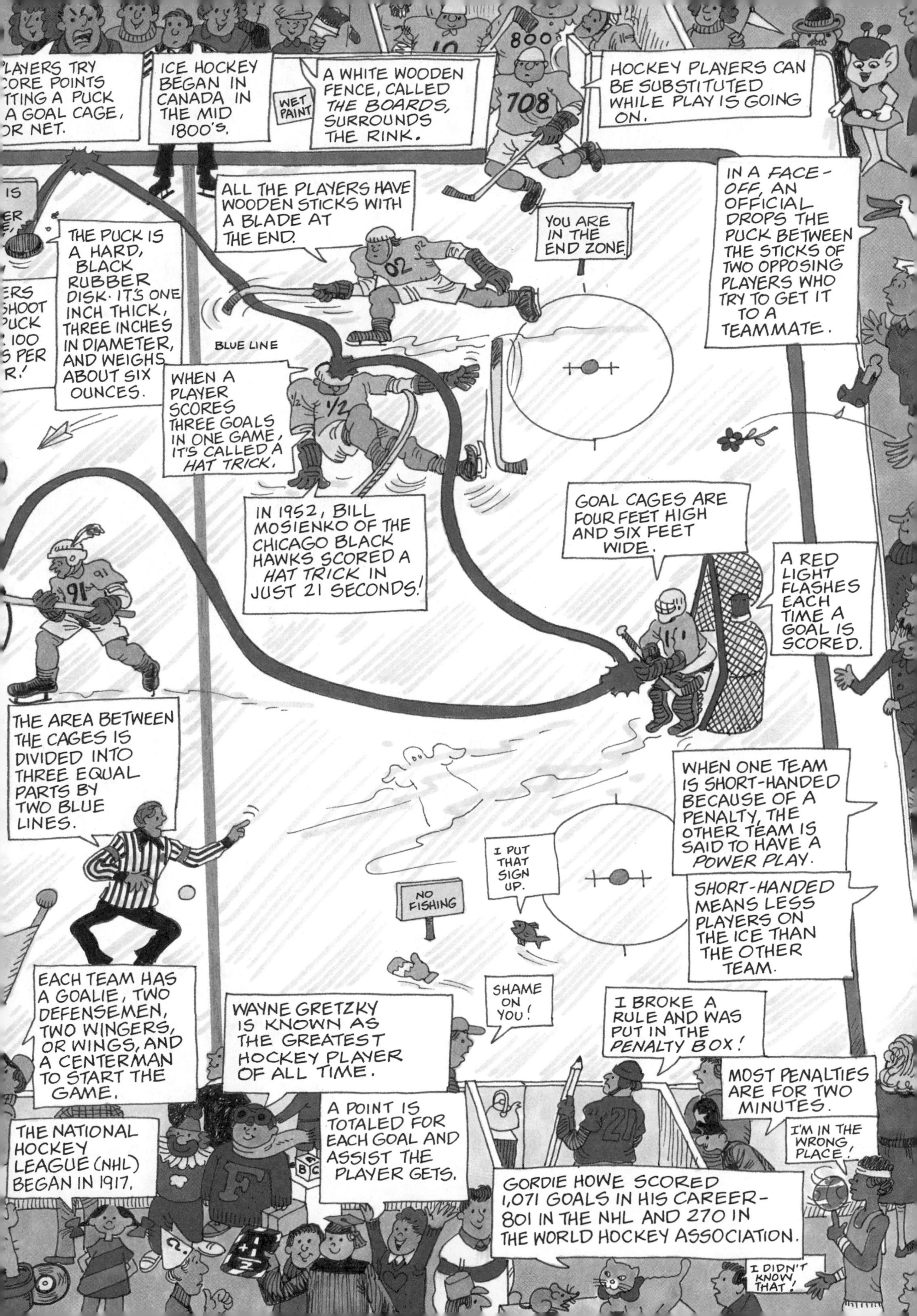

LAYERS TRY CORE POINTS TTING A PUCK A GOAL CAGE, OR NET.
ICE HOCKEY BEGAN IN CANADA IN THE MID 1800'S.
WET PAINT
A WHITE WOODEN FENCE, CALLED *THE BOARDS*, SURROUNDS THE RINK.
800
708
HOCKEY PLAYERS CAN BE SUBSTITUTED WHILE PLAY IS GOING ON.
ALL THE PLAYERS HAVE WOODEN STICKS WITH A BLADE AT THE END.
YOU ARE IN THE END ZONE.
IN A *FACE-OFF*, AN OFFICIAL DROPS THE PUCK BETWEEN THE STICKS OF TWO OPPOSING PLAYERS WHO TRY TO GET IT TO A TEAMMATE.
THE PUCK IS A HARD, BLACK RUBBER DISK. IT'S ONE INCH THICK, THREE INCHES IN DIAMETER, AND WEIGHS ABOUT SIX OUNCES.
02
BLUE LINE
WHEN A PLAYER SCORES THREE GOALS IN ONE GAME, IT'S CALLED A *HAT TRICK*.
1/2
IN 1952, BILL MOSIENKO OF THE CHICAGO BLACK HAWKS SCORED A *HAT TRICK* IN JUST 21 SECONDS!
GOAL CAGES ARE FOUR FEET HIGH AND SIX FEET WIDE.
A RED LIGHT FLASHES EACH TIME A GOAL IS SCORED.
91
THE AREA BETWEEN THE CAGES IS DIVIDED INTO THREE EQUAL PARTS BY TWO BLUE LINES.
WHEN ONE TEAM IS SHORT-HANDED BECAUSE OF A PENALTY, THE OTHER TEAM IS SAID TO HAVE A *POWER PLAY*.
I PUT THAT SIGN UP.
NO FISHING
SHORT-HANDED MEANS LESS PLAYERS ON THE ICE THAN THE OTHER TEAM.
EACH TEAM HAS A GOALIE, TWO DEFENSEMEN, TWO WINGERS, OR WINGS, AND A CENTERMAN TO START THE GAME.
WAYNE GRETZKY IS KNOWN AS THE GREATEST HOCKEY PLAYER OF ALL TIME.
SHAME ON YOU!
I BROKE A RULE AND WAS PUT IN THE *PENALTY BOX*!
MOST PENALTIES ARE FOR TWO MINUTES.
I'M IN THE WRONG PLACE!
21
THE NATIONAL HOCKEY LEAGUE (NHL) BEGAN IN 1917.
A POINT IS TOTALED FOR EACH GOAL AND ASSIST THE PLAYER GETS.
F
GORDIE HOWE SCORED 1,071 GOALS IN HIS CAREER-801 IN THE NHL AND 270 IN THE WORLD HOCKEY ASSOCIATION.
I DIDN'T KNOW THAT!

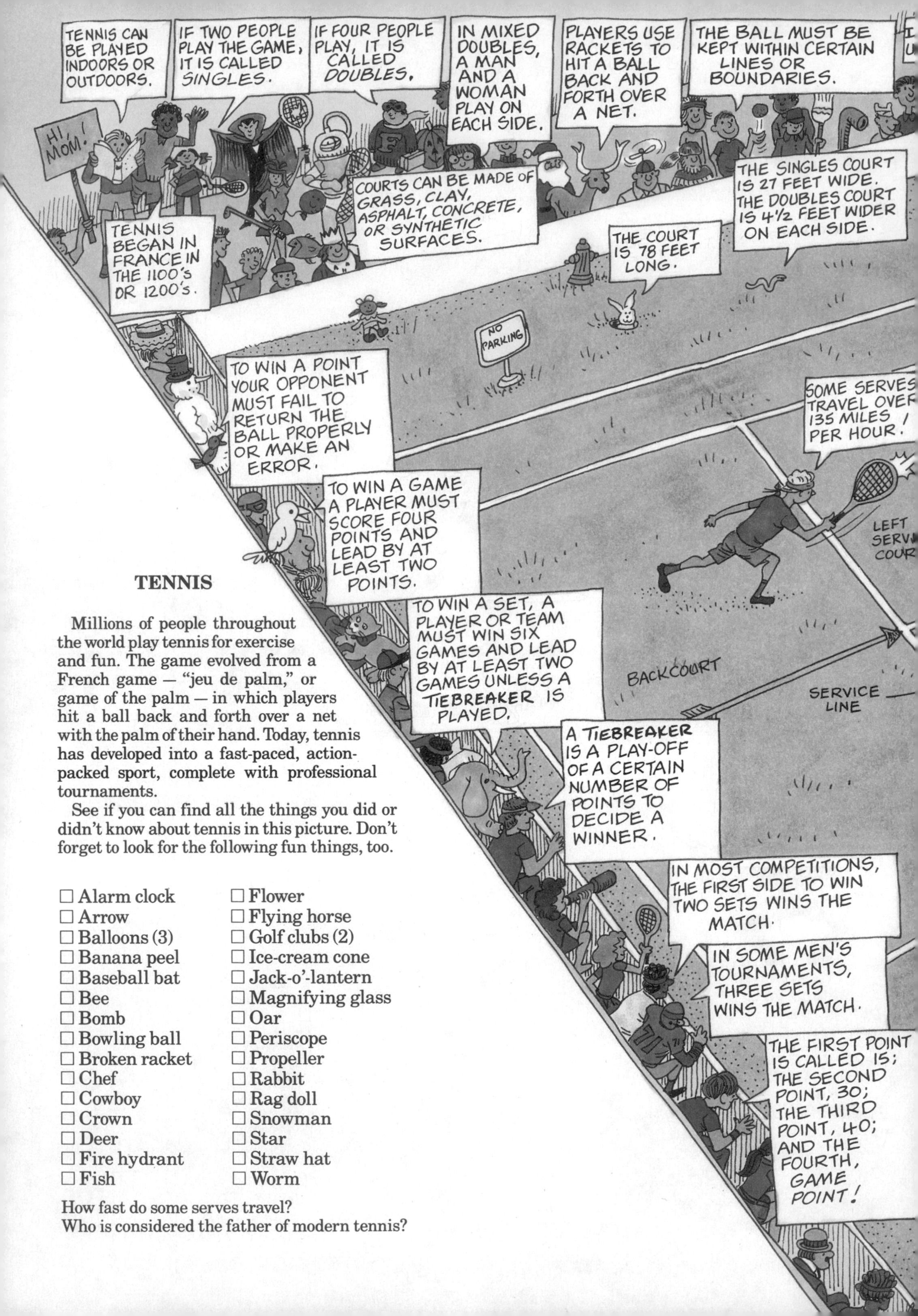

TENNIS

Millions of people throughout the world play tennis for exercise and fun. The game evolved from a French game — "jeu de palm," or game of the palm — in which players hit a ball back and forth over a net with the palm of their hand. Today, tennis has developed into a fast-paced, action-packed sport, complete with professional tournaments.

See if you can find all the things you did or didn't know about tennis in this picture. Don't forget to look for the following fun things, too.

- ☐ Alarm clock
- ☐ Arrow
- ☐ Balloons (3)
- ☐ Banana peel
- ☐ Baseball bat
- ☐ Bee
- ☐ Bomb
- ☐ Bowling ball
- ☐ Broken racket
- ☐ Chef
- ☐ Cowboy
- ☐ Crown
- ☐ Deer
- ☐ Fire hydrant
- ☐ Fish
- ☐ Flower
- ☐ Flying horse
- ☐ Golf clubs (2)
- ☐ Ice-cream cone
- ☐ Jack-o'-lantern
- ☐ Magnifying glass
- ☐ Oar
- ☐ Periscope
- ☐ Propeller
- ☐ Rabbit
- ☐ Rag doll
- ☐ Snowman
- ☐ Star
- ☐ Straw hat
- ☐ Worm

How fast do some serves travel?
Who is considered the father of modern tennis?

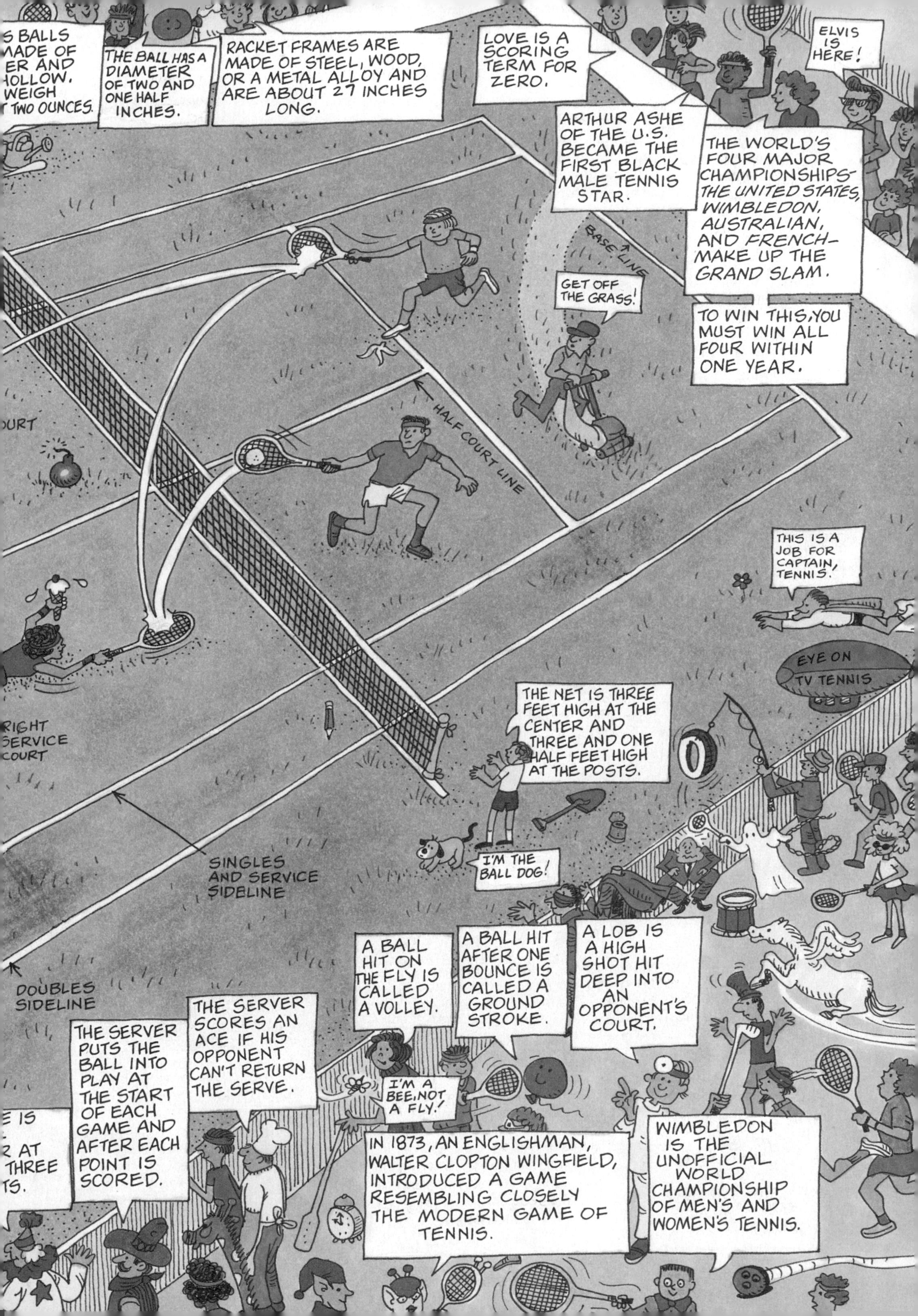
S BALLS
MADE OF
ER AND
HOLLOW.
WEIGH
T TWO OUNCES.
THE BALL HAS A DIAMETER OF TWO AND ONE HALF INCHES.
RACKET FRAMES ARE MADE OF STEEL, WOOD, OR A METAL ALLOY AND ARE ABOUT 27 INCHES LONG.
LOVE IS A SCORING TERM FOR ZERO.
ELVIS IS HERE!
ARTHUR ASHE OF THE U.S. BECAME THE FIRST BLACK MALE TENNIS STAR.
THE WORLD'S FOUR MAJOR CHAMPIONSHIPS- THE UNITED STATES, WIMBLEDON, AUSTRALIAN, AND FRENCH- MAKE UP THE GRAND SLAM.
TO WIN THIS, YOU MUST WIN ALL FOUR WITHIN ONE YEAR.
BASE LINE
GET OFF THE GRASS!
HALF COURT LINE
OURT
THIS IS A JOB FOR CAPTAIN, TENNIS.
EYE ON TV TENNIS
THE NET IS THREE FEET HIGH AT THE CENTER AND THREE AND ONE HALF FEET HIGH AT THE POSTS.
RIGHT SERVICE COURT
I'M THE BALL DOG!
SINGLES AND SERVICE SIDELINE
DOUBLES SIDELINE
A BALL HIT ON THE FLY IS CALLED A VOLLEY.
A BALL HIT AFTER ONE BOUNCE IS CALLED A GROUND STROKE.
A LOB IS A HIGH SHOT HIT DEEP INTO AN OPPONENT'S COURT.
THE SERVER SCORES AN ACE IF HIS OPPONENT CAN'T RETURN THE SERVE.
THE SERVER PUTS THE BALL INTO PLAY AT THE START OF EACH GAME AND AFTER EACH POINT IS SCORED.
I'M A BEE, NOT A FLY!
E IS
R AT
THREE
TS.
IN 1873, AN ENGLISHMAN, WALTER CLOPTON WINGFIELD, INTRODUCED A GAME RESEMBLING CLOSELY THE MODERN GAME OF TENNIS.
WIMBLEDON IS THE UNOFFICIAL WORLD CHAMPIONSHIP OF MEN'S AND WOMEN'S TENNIS.

MARTIAL ARTS

The martial arts are more than a method of combat. They are important as a means of developing one's physical, spiritual, and mental being.

Centuries ago, Buddhist monks roamed throughout Asia spreading their philosophy and knowledge of the martial arts. Each culture modified this philosophy to suit its needs, thus developing new martial arts techniques.

See if you can find all the things you did or didn't know about martial arts in this picture. Don't forget to look for the following fun things, too.

- ☐ Anchor
- ☐ Artist
- ☐ Banana peel
- ☐ Bird
- ☐ Black belt ghost
- ☐ Bone
- ☐ Book
- ☐ Book of matches
- ☐ Boxer
- ☐ Carrot
- ☐ Chef's hat
- ☐ Clown
- ☐ Crown
- ☐ Football
- ☐ Jack-o'-lantern
- ☐ Karate rat
- ☐ Lost boot
- ☐ Lost glove
- ☐ Lost mitten
- ☐ Magnet
- ☐ Mummy
- ☐ Ninja bunny
- ☐ Piggy bank
- ☐ Saw
- ☐ Scarecrow
- ☐ Skateboard
- ☐ Snake
- ☐ Speaker
- ☐ Stopwatch
- ☐ Wizard
- ☐ Yo-yo

What is Tae Kwon Do?

How do karate students toughen their hands and feet?

KARATE IS A FORM OF UNARMED COMBAT IN WHICH A PERSON KICKS OR STRIKES WITH HANDS, ELBOWS, FEET, OR KNEES.
THERE ARE FOUR MAJOR TYPES OF KARATE – CHINESE, JAPANESE, KOREAN, AND OKINAWAN.
THE JAPANESE WORD FOR KARATE MEANS EMPTY HAND, TAKEN FROM "KARA," EMPTY, AND "TE," HAND.
TAE KWON DO IS THE KOREAN ART OF SELF-DEFENSE. IT EMPHASIZES KICKING. IT MEANS "FOOT-HAND ART."
TAE KWON DO COMBINES PHYSICAL AND MENTAL DISCIPLINE WITH A DEEP PHILOSOPHY.
I'M KARATE RAT.
FOUR JUDGES-ONE SEATED AT EACH CORNER
•ARBITRATOR
•TIMEKEEPER
•RECORDKEEPER
•ADMINISTRATOR
STARTING LINE
REFEREE
STARTING LINE
CHINESE KARATE IS CALLED KUNG FU.
IT USES FLOWING, CIRCULAR MOTIONS.
THE BELT DENOTES THE WEARER'S RANK.
BEGINNERS WEAR WHITE.
EXPERTS WEAR BLACK.
BROWN, GREEN, AND PURPLE SIGNIFY INTERMEDIATE RANKS.
THE UNIFORM IS CALLED KARATEGI.
MY PANTS SPLIT!
I HAVE A BLACK BELT.

HEN KARATE STUDENTS RACTICE THEY STOP SHORT OF HITTING THEIR OPPONENT, OR TOUCH THEM LIGHTLY. THIS AVOIDS SERIOUS INJURY.
A DACHI IS A STANCE OR WAY OF STANDING.
THERE ARE DIFFERENT KINDS OF STANCES...
THE READY STANCE, THE CAT STANCE, THE BACK STANCE, THE SIDE STANCE, THE FORWARD STANCE, AND THE HORSEBACK-RIDING STANCE.
THIS IS A FRONT STANCE.
KICKING TECHNIQUES INCLUDE THE HOOK KICK, THE FRONT KICK, THE SIDE KICK, AND THE ROUNDHOUSE KICK.
ONLY IKES FULL CE IN SELF-FENSE.
THIS IS A KNIFE HAND BLOCK.
FLYING FRONT KICK
ND PLAYS MPORTANT E IN KARATE. N AN ATTACKER KES, HE YELLS H!" OR "YIAH!" T MAXIMUM CE INTO THE W.
YOU PUNCH WITH THE KNUCKLES OF THE FIRST TWO FINGERS.
SIDE KICK
ROUNDHOUSE KICKS
STRIKING USES OTHER PARTS OF THE HAND.
NER T IS N AS YA.
I GET A KICK OUT OF THIS.
I WANT A PEANUT BUTTER SANDWICH!
RIGHT AWAY!
N'T W T?
A SENSEI IS A KARATE TEACHER.
A ZUKI IS A PUNCH.
A UKE IS A BLOCK.
A GERI IS A KICK.
A DOJO IS A KARATE TRAINING HALL.
NOW I KNOW IT!
CRUNCH!
CHUNG KOOK-HYUN OF SOUTH KOREA HAS WON FOUR WORLD TAE KWON DO CHAMPIONSHIPS.
I FORGOT MY SHOES.
ME, TOO!
I'M KARATE TURTLE.
I'M NINJA BUNNY.
TRAINING ENDS WITH A RITSU REI OR STANDING BOW. THIS SHOWS RESPECT TO THE OPPONENT OR TEACHER.
JAPANESE AIKIDO IS A NON-COMPETITIVE MARTIAL ART.
MATCH SUALLY ASTS WO INUTES.
THREE POINTS WINS A MATCH. IF NO ONE HAS SCORED THREE POINTS, THE ONE WITH THE MOST POINTS WINS.
A KATA COMPETITION USES A PREARRANGED SEQUENCE OF KICKS, BLOCKS, AND PUNCHES TO DEMONSTRATE SKILL.
YOU BROKE THE BOARD!
THEY DON'T NEED ME!

TRACK AND FIELD

Track and field is a sport in which men and women compete in athletic events featuring running, throwing, and jumping. Track events consist of a series of races over various distances ranging from 60 meters to a marathon. Field events measure an athlete's ability to throw and jump.

See if you can find all the things you did or didn't know about track and field in this picture. Don't forget to look for the following fun things, too.

- ☐ Ball of yarn
- ☐ Balloon
- ☐ Birdcage
- ☐ Bomb
- ☐ Candle
- ☐ Chef's hat
- ☐ Count Dracula
- ☐ Deliveryman
- ☐ Duck
- ☐ Elephant
- ☐ Fish
- ☐ Flying bat
- ☐ Football player
- ☐ Helicopter
- ☐ Ice-cream cone
- ☐ Mummy
- ☐ Ostrich
- ☐ Painted egg
- ☐ Periscope
- ☐ Pig
- ☐ Rabbit
- ☐ Roller skater
- ☐ Snake
- ☐ Surfboard
- ☐ Thief
- ☐ Tinman
- ☐ Tuba
- ☐ Turtle
- ☐ Umbrella
- ☐ Weightlifter

How long is a marathon?

Name the four throwing events.

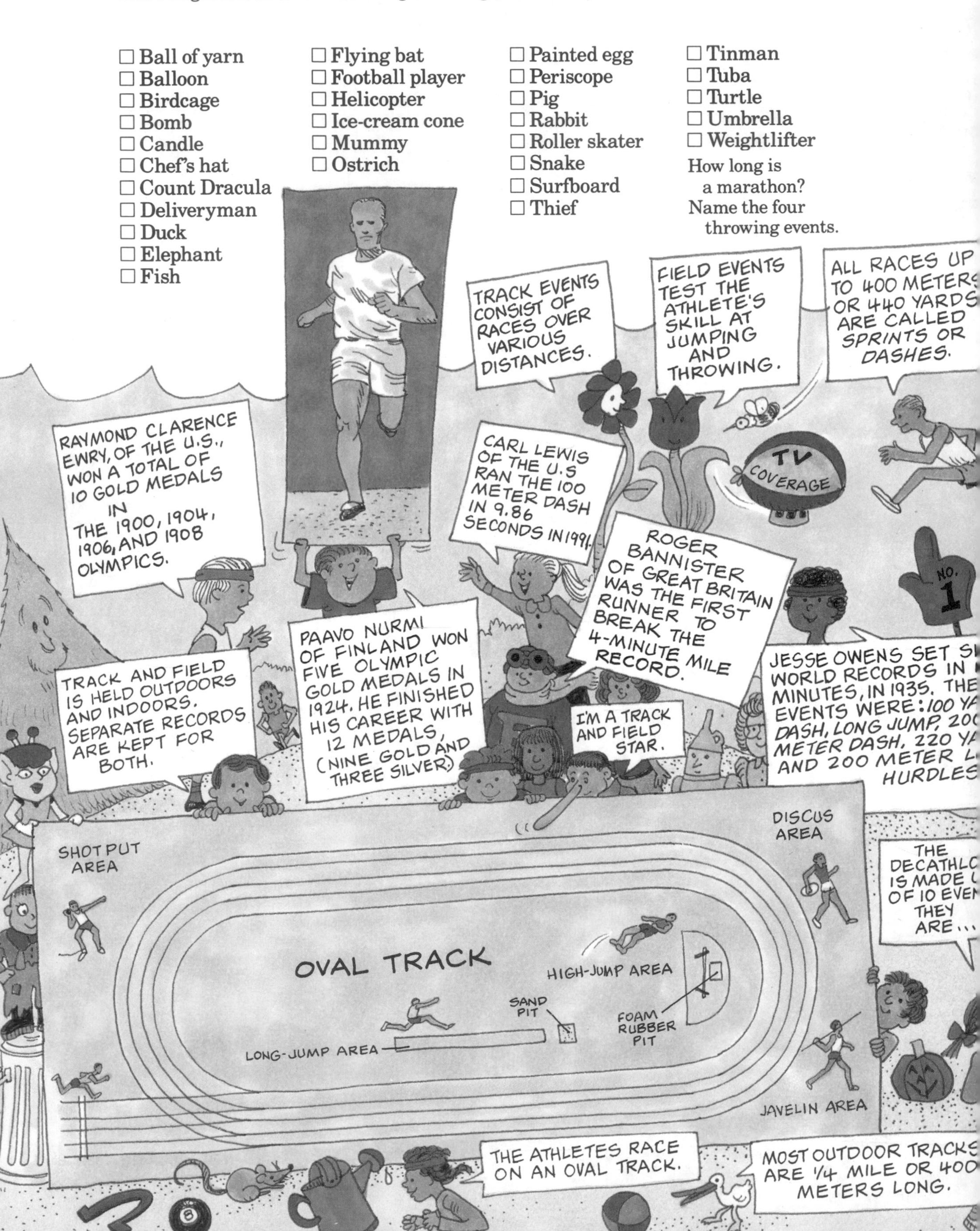

IGH JUMPERS AND
OLE VAULTERS
AND IN A PIT OF
AWDUST OR FOAM
UBBER OR ON AN
R-INFLATED PAD.
IF THE BAR COMES OFF THE POLES DURING THE JUMP OR VAULT IT COUNTS AS A MISS.
THE SHOT IS A 16 POUND METAL BALL.
DISCUS IS A
ATTER-SHAPED
BJECT MADE OF
ETAL AND WOOD,
EASURING 8 3/4
CHES IN DIAMETER
D WEIGHING AT
EAST 4 POUNDS
5 1/2 OUNCES.
A HAMMER IS A METAL BALL ATTACHED TO ONE END OF A STEEL WIRE. A HANDLE IS ON THE OTHER END. IT WEIGHS 16 POUNDS.
THE JAVELIN IS MADE OF METAL OR WOOD, AND MEASURES BETWEEN 8 FEET 6 1/4 INCHES AND 8 FEET 10 1/4 INCHES LONG, AND WEIGHS AT LEAST 28 OUNCES.
DLE-DISTANCE
ES COVER FROM
METERS OR
YARDS TO
METERS OR
MILE.
OVER A MILE OR 1500 METERS ARE LONG DISTANCE RACES.
RELAY RUNNERS CAN'T RUN UNTIL THEY HAVE THE BATON.
A RELAY TEAM HAS 4 MEMBERS. EACH RUNS PART OF THE RACE.
WHERE'S THE FIELD?
DON'T STOP
ERE'S
HE
CK?
OOPS!
THIS WAY
I'M THE MARATHON SPIRIT.
THE MARATHON IS 26 MILES, 385 YARDS.
OVER 25,000 RUNNERS TAKE PART IN THE NEW YORK CITY MARATHON EACH YEAR.
COMING THROUGH! HOT PIZZA!
BELAYNEH DENSIMO OF ETHIOPIA RAN THE MARATHON IN 2 HOURS, 6 MINUTES, 50 SECONDS.
HI, MOM!
CAN McLEAN
SCOTLAND RAN
100 METER
H IN 21.7
ONDS AT THE
OF 92!
THE LONG JUMP
THE HIGH JUMP
THE SHOT PUT
DISCUS
THE POLE VAULT
THE 110 METER HURDLES
JAVELIN
THE 400 METER RUN
THE 1500 METER RUN
READY? SET? GO!!
TOO FAST FOR ME.

FAMOUS PEOPLE AND PLACES

Search and find lots of interesting facts about:

- Walt Disney World
- Sacagawea
- Neil Armstrong
- Washington, D.C.
- Joan of Arc
- Jacques Cousteau
- New York City
- The Pyramids and the Great Sphinx
- Leonardo da Vinci
- The Grand Canyon and the Rocky Mountains
- Christopher Columbus

WHAT WAS THE FIRST SOUND CARTOON?
WALT DISNEY'S "STEAMBOAT WILLIE," IN 1928.
MICKEY MOUSE WAS THE STAR AND WALT DISNEY WAS MICKEY'S VOICE.
I WANT TO SEE THE "HALL OF PRESIDENTS."
LIBERTY SQUARE
FRONTIERLAND
ME, TOO!
I LIKE "THE HAUNTED MANSION."
I LIKE "PIRATES OF THE CARIBBEAN."
ADVENTURELAND
I'M A PLUTO FAN.
"THAT'S CINDERELLA'S CASTLE."
IT'S 180 FEET TALL.
I CAN FLY!
DISNEY MAKES LIVE ACTION AND ANIMATED MOTION PICTURES.
THERE IS A HUGE NETWORK OF ROOMS AND PATHWAYS UNDERNEATH DISNEY WORLD!
I'M LOOKING FOR THE "JUNGLE BOAT RIDE."
THIS IS 43 SQUARE MILES OF FAMILY FUN.
MARY POPPINS COMBINED BOTH LIVE ACTION AND CARTOONS.
IT'S FOR THE EMPLOYEES TO STORE AND DELIVER FOOD AND MERCHANDISE.
WHO ORDERED PIZZA?
WHAT WAS THE FIRST FULL-LENGTH DISNEY CARTOON?
HI!
THERE'S ALSO A COMPUTER CENTER BENEATH MAIN STREET THAT CONTROLS MANY OF THE ATTRACTIONS AND SERVICES.
IT'S LOCATED IN ORLANDO, FLORIDA.
IT OPENED IN 1971.
WE SHOULD HAVE A "WHERE ARE THEY?" LAND.
THERE'S MICKEY!
GET ME OFF.
WALT DISNEY WAS AN ANIMATOR.
AN ANIMATOR IS AN ARTIST WHO DRAWS MOVIE CARTOONS.
IT'S A GREAT DAY.
VISIT US!
TUESDAY IS THE BUSIEST DAY.
MINNIE
MICKEY
MAIN STREET, U.S.A.

WALT DISNEY WORLD

Walt Disney World is the fulfillment of Walt Disney's dream. He ted to create the ultimate amusement park where adults and children d have fun together. Today, Walt Disney World in Florida is the most ılar man-made attraction in the world and is visited by thousands of ıle every day.

See if you can find all the things you did or didn't know about Walt ıey World in this picture. Don't forget to look for the following fun gs, too!

- ☐ Arrow
- ☐ Balloon
- ☐ Cake
- ☐ Chef's hat
- ☐ Clown
- ☐ Crown
- ☐ Drummer
- ☐ Elephants (2)
- ☐ Fish
- ☐ Football
- ☐ Football player
- ☐ Ghost
- ☐ Hammock
- ☐ Hearts (3)
- ☐ Horse
- ☐ Horseshoe
- ☐ Ice-cream cone
- ☐ Jack-o'-lantern
- ☐ Kite
- ☐ Ladder
- ☐ Lion
- ☐ Magnifying glass
- ☐ Pencil
- ☐ Penguin
- ☐ Snowman
- ☐ Telescope
- ☐ TV set

Who starred in "Steamboat Willie"?
On what day is Walt Disney World busiest?

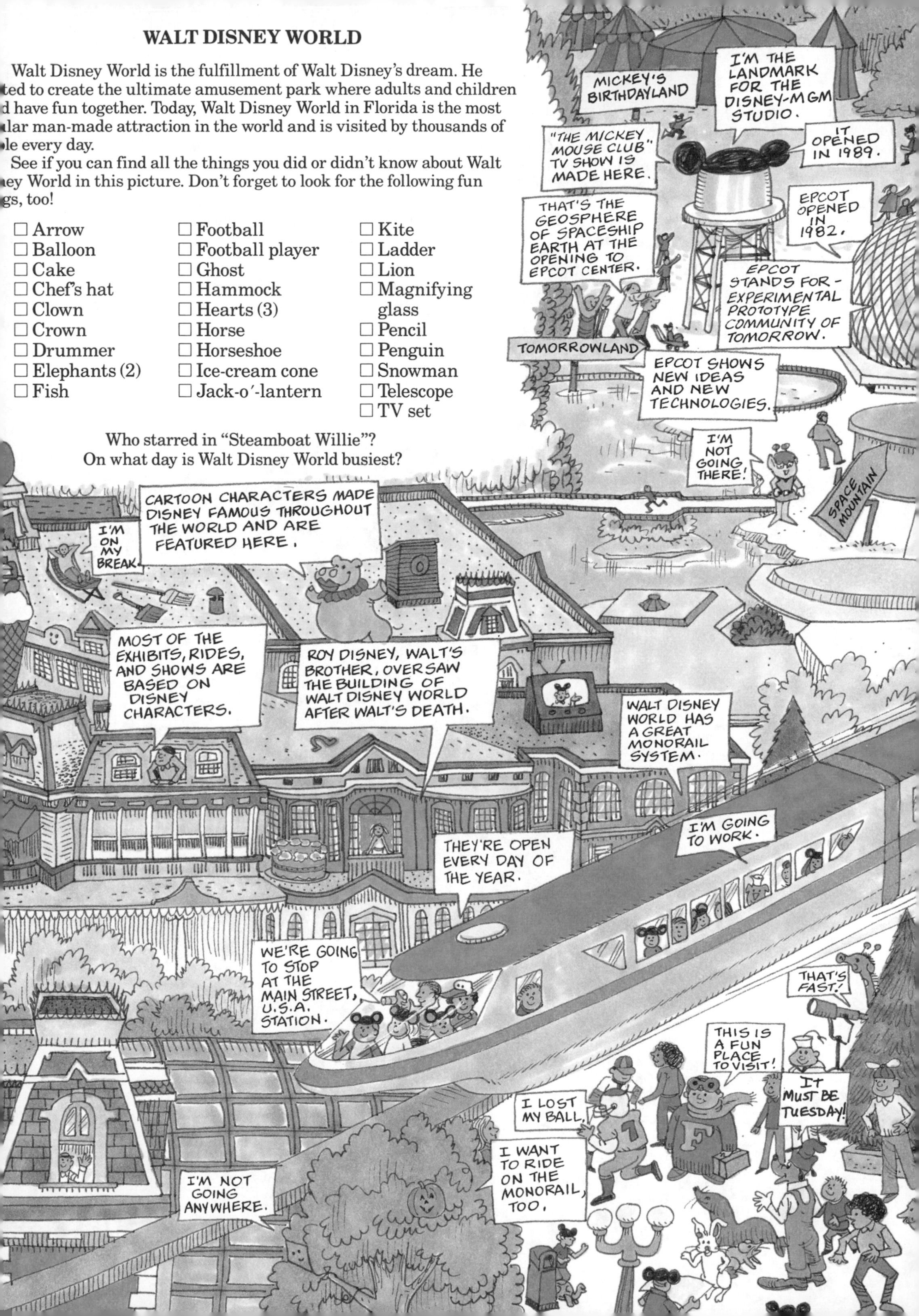

SACAGAWEA

Sacagawea (SAK-uh-juh-WEE-uh) was born among the Shoshone (show-SHOW-nee) Indians. As a young girl she was captured by an enemy tribe and sold as a slave to a trader who joined the Lewis and Clark expedition. Sacagawea became the principle guide for the expedition as they made their way across western lands to the Pacific Ocean and back again in 1804 and 1805. Historians have called Sacagawea one of the six most important American women of all time.

See if you can find all the things you did or didn't know about Sacagawea in this picture. Don't forget to look for the following fun things, too!

- ☐ Armadillo
- ☐ Arrows (2)
- ☐ Baby
- ☐ Bears (2)
- ☐ Beaver
- ☐ Bow
- ☐ Buffalo
- ☐ Coyote
- ☐ Deer
- ☐ Drum
- ☐ Eagle
- ☐ Egg
- ☐ Flying bat
- ☐ Flying saucer
- ☐ Frog
- ☐ Groundhog
- ☐ Heart
- ☐ Lost boot
- ☐ Moose
- ☐ Mountain goat
- ☐ Mushroom
- ☐ Owl
- ☐ Rabbits (3)
- ☐ Sailboat
- ☐ Skunk
- ☐ Snake
- ☐ Spear
- ☐ Turtle
- ☐ Wild turkey

What does Sacagawea mea
Why did she agree
guide Lewis and

WE'RE LOOKING FOR LAURA.
I NEVER SAW THEM BEFORE.
WE STARTED FROM ST. LOUIS, MISSOURI, IN MAY, 1804.
SHE JOINED US AT FORT MANDAN, NEAR WASHBURN, NORTH DAKOTA.
THE FIRST PART OUR JOURNEY ON THE ISSISSIPPI RIVER...
...WE RAN INTO A STORM THAT CAPSIZED A CANOE.
SACAGAWEA SAVED THE MAPS, MEDICINE, AND OTHER VALUABLE SUPPLIES BEFORE THE CANOE SANK!
SHE USED NEEDLES MADE FROM BIRD BONES TO SEW TORN CLOTHES.
SHE MADE MEDICINES FROM WILD PLANTS AND HERBS.
SHE ALSO MADE CLOTHES AND SHOES FROM BUCKSKIN FOR US.
DID I FORGET ANYTHING?
THE PACIFIC OCEAN IS THE LARGEST OF THE FOUR OCEANS.
I'M A WILD TURKEY!
MY FEET HURT.
I NEED A HAIR CUT!
CONGRESS APPROVED $2,500.00 FOR THIS EXPEDITION!
THERE SHE IS.
SHE'S VERY BRAVE.
SHE WAS CAPTURED BY AN ENEMY TRIBE, THE MINITAREES.
OUCH!!
SHE WAS SOLD TO A FRENCH-CANADIAN TRADER WHO BECAME HER HUSBAND.
SHE'S GUIDING OUR EXPEDITION BECAUSE SHE WANTS TO SEE THE "BIG WATERS."
I NEED A SHAVE.
THAT'S THE PACIFIC OCEAN.
SHE NAMED HER BABY "POMP" WHICH MEANS FIRST BORN.
A NOISY GROUP!
YOU WOKE ME UP!
GO FOR THIS, GO FOR THAT!
LEWIS AND CLARK WILL BE THE FIRST WHITE MEN TO MAKE THE TRIP ACROSS THE U.S. FROM THE ATLANTIC TO THE PACIFIC OCEANS.
DO NOT DISTURB
DID THEY BRING ANY HONEY ALONG?
DO NOT PICK FLOWERS
Z-Z-Z-Z-Z!
I LIKE TO WAIL ALONG THE TRAIL!

NEIL ARMSTRONG

Neil Alden Armstrong is one of the United States' most famous astronauts. On July 20, 1969, Armstrong and fellow astronaut Edwin "Buzz" Aldrin, Jr., landed the Apollo 11 lunar module on the moon's surface. Armstrong became the first person to set foot on the moon.

See if you can find all the things you did or didn't know about Neil Armstrong and the moon in this picture. Don't forget to look for the following fun things, too!

- ☐ Balloon
- ☐ Banana peel
- ☐ Bird
- ☐ Cactus
- ☐ Can
- ☐ Cloud
- ☐ Earth
- ☐ Firecracker
- ☐ Fire hydrant
- ☐ Fish (3)
- ☐ Flashlight
- ☐ Flying saucer
- ☐ Heart
- ☐ Hot-air balloon
- ☐ Hot dog
- ☐ Ice-cream cone
- ☐ Key
- ☐ Kite
- ☐ Lamp
- ☐ Mouse
- ☐ Paper airplane
- ☐ Pencil
- ☐ Policeman
- ☐ Scale
- ☐ School bus
- ☐ Sock
- ☐ Superhero
- ☐ Top hat
- ☐ Umbrella
- ☐ Wagon wheel

What did Neil Armstrong say when he first set foot on the moon's surface?

About how much would you weigh on the moon?

TIME FOR LUNCH.
THE MOON IS 1/4 THE SIZE OF EARTH!
IT HAS 1/6 THE GRAVITY OF EARTH.
NEIL BECAME AN ASTRONAUT IN 1962.
HE WAS A NAVY PILOT FROM 1949 TO 1952.
I WAS AN ASTRONAUT IN OUR YEAR 2707 1/4.
FOR SALE
I DIDN'T KNOW THAT!
ARMSTRONG MADE HIS FIRST SPACE FLIGHT IN 1966 ABOARD GEMINI 8.
I SAW THAT!
HE AND DAVID SCOTT PERFORMED THE FIRST SUCCESSFUL JOINING TOGETHER OF TWO VEHICLES IN SPACE.
TO FIND YOUR MOON WEIGHT, DIVIDE YOUR WEIGHT ON EARTH BY SIX.
THE MOON IS NOT MADE OF CHEESE.
MADE IN THE U.S.A.
CRATERS, LIKE ME, WERE FORMED BILLIONS OF YEARS AGO BY CRASHING METEORITES.
WHEN THE APOLLO 11 LANDED ON THE MOON, THE IMPACT CAUSED THE MOON'S SURFACE TO VIBRATE!
THE MOON HAS NO LIGHT. IT JUST REFLECTS LIGHT FROM THE SUN.
CRATER FOR RENT!

WASHINGTON, D.C.

George Washington envisioned a city of beauty and stature for the new nation's capital when he chose Pierre L'Enfant, a French architect/engineer, to design it in 1790. Today's Washington, D.C. is certainly that. It has wide, straight avenues, lush parks, towering monuments, and beautiful trees and flowers.

Washington is also the political center of the nation. Here decisions are made in both the White House, the home of the President, and in the Capitol, the home of the Senate and House of Representatives, which affect the lives of millions of people.

This picture shows postcards from a class trip. See if you can find all the things you did or didn't know about Washington, D.C. Don't forget to look for the following fun things, too!

- ☐ Balloon
- ☐ Baseball cap
- ☐ Bird
- ☐ Brush
- ☐ Cactus
- ☐ Fish
- ☐ Fishbowl
- ☐ Flags (3)
- ☐ Flower
- ☐ Headband
- ☐ Key
- ☐ Kite
- ☐ Mouse
- ☐ Painted egg
- ☐ Scarves (2)
- ☐ Star
- ☐ Three-corn hats (2)
- ☐ Top Hat

When did the U.S. government move to Washington, D.C.?

What is the pu of the city of Washington?

STATUE OF A WOMAN, "FREEDOM," IS 19½ FEET TALL AND WEIGHS 7½ TONS.
THE CAPITOL DOME WEIGHS 9 MILLION POUNDS.
I LOVE D.C.
THE ROTUNDA IS A BIG CIRCULAR HALL BENEATH THE CAPITOL DOME.
IT IS DECORATED WITH PAINTINGS AND SCULPTURE SHOWING THE HISTORY OF THE COUNTRY.
OUR CLASS WAS THERE!
WE SAW D.C. FROM UP HERE.
WE WENT TO THE TOP!
THAT'S THE CAPITOL, WHERE THE SENATE AND THE HOUSE OF REPRESENTATIVES MEET.
A CAPITAL IS THE CITY WHERE THE STATE OR NATIONAL GOVERNMENT CONDUCTS BUSINESS.
IN 1814, BRITISH FORCES MARCHED INTO WASHINGTON AND BURNED THE CAPITOL AND THE WHITE HOUSE ALMOST TO THE GROUND.
IT WAS NAMED "THE WHITE HOUSE" BECAUSE OF ALL THE WHITE PAINT USED TO COVER THE SMOKE STAINS AFTER IT WAS BURNED.
THAT'S ME IN THAT PICTURE.
NICE THREE-CORNERED HAT.
THE CITY HAS ONE PURPOSE- GOVERNMENT!
IT WAS NAMED AFTER GEORGE WASHINGTON.
THE U.S. GOVERNMENT MOVED FROM PHILADELPHIA TO WASHINGTON, D.C. IN 1800.
D-IS FOR DISTRICT. C-IS FOR COLUMBIA- WHICH WAS NAMED FOR COLUMBUS.
IT IS A CITY INSIDE A FEDERAL DISTRICT.
GEORGE WASHINGTON CHOSE THE EXACT SITE - WHICH WAS A COMPROMISE BETWEEN THE NORTHERN AND SOUTHERN STATES.
WE SAW A LOT OF THINGS THERE.

E HOUSE WAS T PUBLIC BUILT IN THE OF WASHINGTON.
GEORGE WASHINGTON IS THE ONLY PRESIDENT THAT HAS NOT LIVED HERE.
THIS IS WHERE THE U.S. PRESIDENT LIVES.
THE SMITHSONIAN INSTITUTE WAS FORMED BY JOHN SMITHSON, AN ENGLISHMAN WHO NEVER CAME TO THE U.S.
GET ME DOWN FROM HERE!
E EASTER EGG ROLLING HITE HOUSE
WE WENT TO THE JEFFERSON MEMORIAL - YOU CAN SEE A STATUE OF JEFFERSON HOLDING THE DECLARATION OF INDEPENDENCE HERE.
SUPREME COURT BUILDING - RE 9 JUSTICES D COURT.
THE LINCOLN MEMORIAL HAS 36 MARBLE COLUMNS - ONE FOR EACH STATE OF THE UNION WHICH LINCOLN HELD TOGETHER.
THIS IS ON THE U.S. $5 BILL.
WE SAW DECLARATION OF NDEPENDENCE THE CONSTITUTION THE BILL F RIGHTS- N THE ATIONAL RCHIVES.
VER ELAND HE ONLY DENT TO RRIED IN ITE HOUSE.
UNDERNEATH THE LINCOLN MEMORIAL, PEOPLE HAVE DISCOVERED SECRET CAVES.
JAPAN GAVE WASHINGTON, D.C. 3,000 CHERRY TREES IN 1912.
THE CHERRY BLOSSOM FESTIVAL TAKES PLACE EACH SPRING WHEN THE TREES BLOOM.
EVERY U.S. PRESIDENT BUT WASHINGTON HAS LIVED IN WASHINGTON, D.C.
IN 1964, WASHINGTON RESIDENTS FINALLY WERE GIVEN THE RIGHT TO VOTE FOR PRESIDENT OF THE U.S.
MARYLAND CONTRIBUTED 69 SQUARE MILES AND VIRGINIA, 31 SQUARE MILES OF ITS LAND TO FORM THE DISTRICT OF COLUMBIA.
BUT IN 1846, VIRGINIA ASKED FOR AND GOT ITS LAND BACK.
I DIDN'T KNOW THAT!
WE ALSO SAW FORD'S THEATRE, WHERE LINCOLN WAS SHOT.

JEANNE D'ARC WAS HER NAME IN FRANCE.
THE D'ARC FAMILY WORKED ON A FARM.
THE BURGUNDIANS, ALLIES OF THE ENGLISH, CONTROLLED MUCH OF THE NORTHERN PART OF FRANCE.
GO FOR IT, JOAN!
JOAN WAS BORN IN DOMRÉMY, A VILLAGE IN NORTHERN FRANCE ON JANUARY 16, 1412.
KING CHARLES VII WAS THE RIGHTFUL HEIR TO THE FRENCH THRONE.
CHARLES HAD NEVER BEEN CROWNED BECAUSE THE ENGLISH WERE TRYING TO FORCE THEIR OWN KING ON THE FRENCH!
SOUTHERN FRAN WAS THE ONLY PART OF THE COUNTRY NOT UNDER ENGLIS RULE.
JOAN NEVER LEARNED HOW TO READ OR WRITE.
IN 1429, JOAN LEFT HOME TO SAVE FRANCE. SHE WAS 17 YEARS OLD!
HEY! LET GO!!
I HAVE BASEBALL PRACTICE AFTER THIS.
IT'S MY TURN TO RIDE!
HE FORGOT HIS HORSE.
?
THIS IS THE BEST SCHOOL PLAY ANY FIFTH GRADE CLASS HAS PUT ON!
JOAN HELPED HER MOTHER AND FATHER WITH THE CHORES ON THE FARM.
JOAN'S MOTHER TAUGHT HER HER PRAYERS AND STORIES ABOUT THE SAINTS.
FRANCE AND ENGLAND WERE FIGHTING THE HUNDRED YEARS' WAR DURING THIS TIME.
AT AGE 13 JOAN BECAME VERY RELIGIOUS AND BEGAN TO HAVE VISIONS AND HEAR VOICES.
SHE BE THEY WE THE VOI OF SAIN THEY TO HER TO DRIVE O THE ENG FROM F TO HAV CHARLES CROWNED AND TO F ORLÉAN

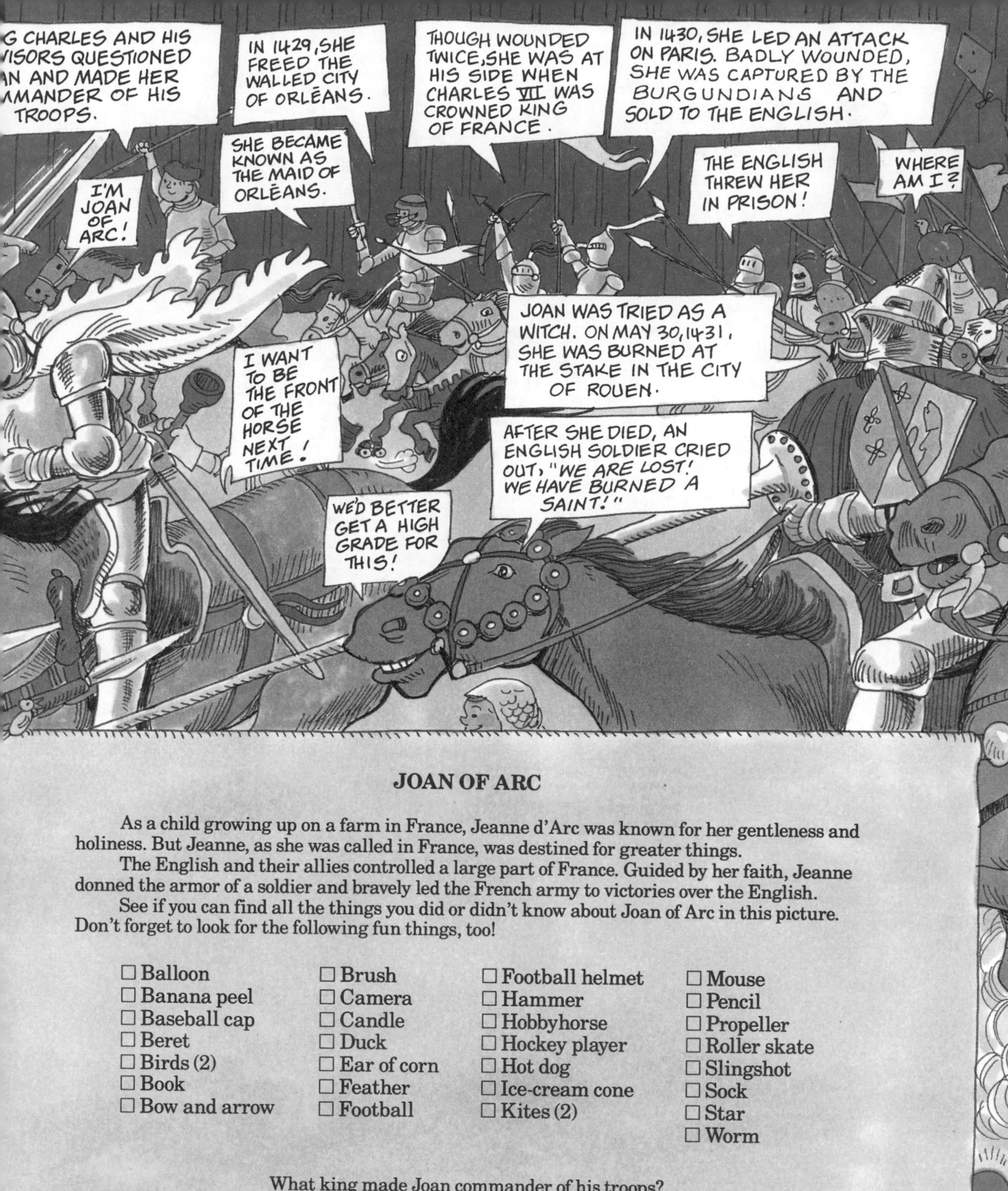

JOAN OF ARC

As a child growing up on a farm in France, Jeanne d'Arc was known for her gentleness and holiness. But Jeanne, as she was called in France, was destined for greater things.

The English and their allies controlled a large part of France. Guided by her faith, Jeanne donned the armor of a soldier and bravely led the French army to victories over the English.

See if you can find all the things you did or didn't know about Joan of Arc in this picture. Don't forget to look for the following fun things, too!

- ☐ Balloon
- ☐ Banana peel
- ☐ Baseball cap
- ☐ Beret
- ☐ Birds (2)
- ☐ Book
- ☐ Bow and arrow
- ☐ Brush
- ☐ Camera
- ☐ Candle
- ☐ Duck
- ☐ Ear of corn
- ☐ Feather
- ☐ Football
- ☐ Football helmet
- ☐ Hammer
- ☐ Hobbyhorse
- ☐ Hockey player
- ☐ Hot dog
- ☐ Ice-cream cone
- ☐ Kites (2)
- ☐ Mouse
- ☐ Pencil
- ☐ Propeller
- ☐ Roller skate
- ☐ Slingshot
- ☐ Sock
- ☐ Star
- ☐ Worm

What king made Joan commander of his troops?

Where was Joan captured?

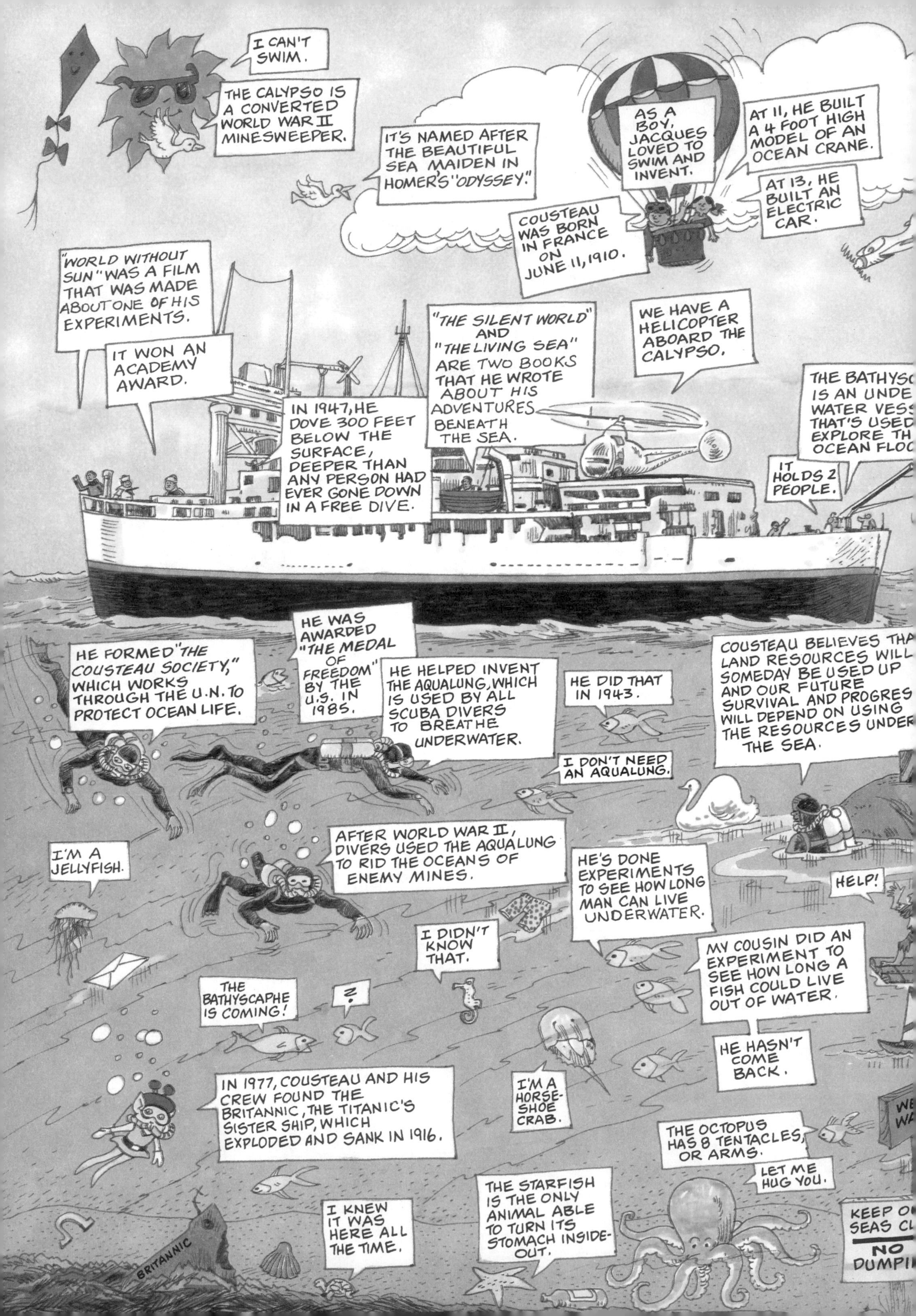
I CAN'T SWIM.
THE CALYPSO IS A CONVERTED WORLD WAR II MINESWEEPER.
IT'S NAMED AFTER THE BEAUTIFUL SEA MAIDEN IN HOMER'S "ODYSSEY."
AS A BOY, JACQUES LOVED TO SWIM AND INVENT.
AT 11, HE BUILT A 4 FOOT HIGH MODEL OF AN OCEAN CRANE.
AT 13, HE BUILT AN ELECTRIC CAR.
COUSTEAU WAS BORN IN FRANCE ON JUNE 11, 1910.
"WORLD WITHOUT SUN" WAS A FILM THAT WAS MADE ABOUT ONE OF HIS EXPERIMENTS.
IT WON AN ACADEMY AWARD.
IN 1947, HE DOVE 300 FEET BELOW THE SURFACE, DEEPER THAN ANY PERSON HAD EVER GONE DOWN IN A FREE DIVE.
"THE SILENT WORLD" AND "THE LIVING SEA" ARE TWO BOOKS THAT HE WROTE ABOUT HIS ADVENTURES BENEATH THE SEA.
WE HAVE A HELICOPTER ABOARD THE CALYPSO.
THE BATHYSC IS AN UNDE WATER VESS THAT'S USED EXPLORE TH OCEAN FLOO
IT HOLDS 2 PEOPLE.
HE FORMED "THE COUSTEAU SOCIETY," WHICH WORKS THROUGH THE U.N. TO PROTECT OCEAN LIFE.
HE WAS AWARDED "THE MEDAL OF FREEDOM" BY THE U.S. IN 1985.
HE HELPED INVENT THE AQUALUNG, WHICH IS USED BY ALL SCUBA DIVERS TO BREATHE UNDERWATER.
HE DID THAT IN 1943.
COUSTEAU BELIEVES THA LAND RESOURCES WILL SOMEDAY BE USED UP AND OUR FUTURE SURVIVAL AND PROGRES WILL DEPEND ON USING THE RESOURCES UNDER THE SEA.
I DON'T NEED AN AQUALUNG.
I'M A JELLYFISH.
AFTER WORLD WAR II, DIVERS USED THE AQUALUNG TO RID THE OCEANS OF ENEMY MINES.
HE'S DONE EXPERIMENTS TO SEE HOW LONG MAN CAN LIVE UNDERWATER.
HELP!
I DIDN'T KNOW THAT.
MY COUSIN DID AN EXPERIMENT TO SEE HOW LONG A FISH COULD LIVE OUT OF WATER.
THE BATHYSCAPHE IS COMING!
?
HE HASN'T COME BACK.
IN 1977, COUSTEAU AND HIS CREW FOUND THE BRITANNIC, THE TITANIC'S SISTER SHIP, WHICH EXPLODED AND SANK IN 1916.
I'M A HORSE-SHOE CRAB.
THE OCTOPUS HAS 8 TENTACLES, OR ARMS.
LET ME HUG YOU.
I KNEW IT WAS HERE ALL THE TIME.
THE STARFISH IS THE ONLY ANIMAL ABLE TO TURN ITS STOMACH INSIDE-OUT.
BRITANNIC
KEEP O SEAS CL
NO DUMPI

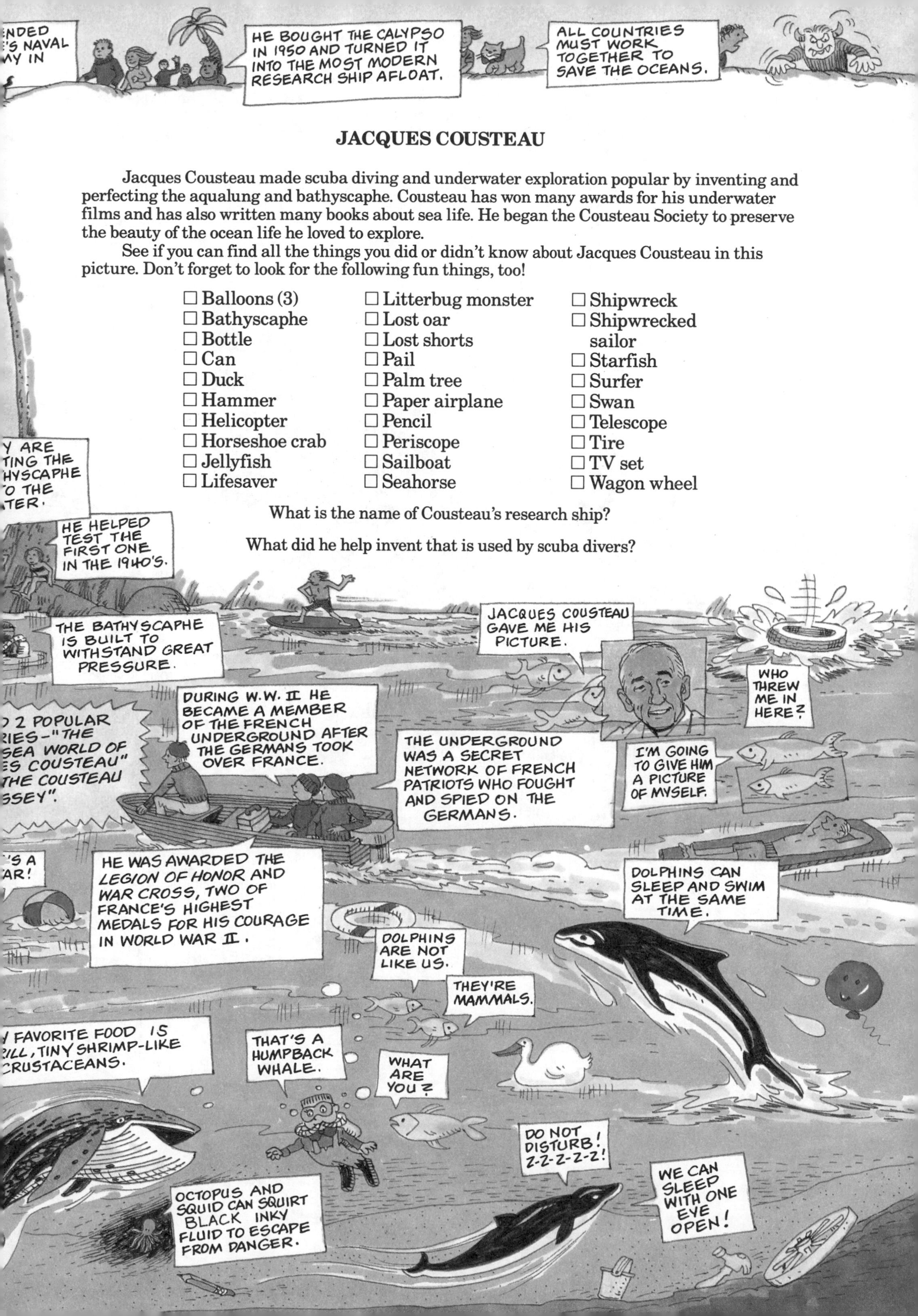

JACQUES COUSTEAU

Jacques Cousteau made scuba diving and underwater exploration popular by inventing and perfecting the aqualung and bathyscaphe. Cousteau has won many awards for his underwater films and has also written many books about sea life. He began the Cousteau Society to preserve the beauty of the ocean life he loved to explore.

See if you can find all the things you did or didn't know about Jacques Cousteau in this picture. Don't forget to look for the following fun things, too!

- ☐ Balloons (3)
- ☐ Bathyscaphe
- ☐ Bottle
- ☐ Can
- ☐ Duck
- ☐ Hammer
- ☐ Helicopter
- ☐ Horseshoe crab
- ☐ Jellyfish
- ☐ Lifesaver
- ☐ Litterbug monster
- ☐ Lost oar
- ☐ Lost shorts
- ☐ Pail
- ☐ Palm tree
- ☐ Paper airplane
- ☐ Pencil
- ☐ Periscope
- ☐ Sailboat
- ☐ Seahorse
- ☐ Shipwreck
- ☐ Shipwrecked sailor
- ☐ Starfish
- ☐ Surfer
- ☐ Swan
- ☐ Telescope
- ☐ Tire
- ☐ TV set
- ☐ Wagon wheel

What is the name of Cousteau's research ship?

What did he help invent that is used by scuba divers?

NEW YORK CITY

New York City is the largest city in the United States and the fifth largest in the world. It is a universal center for art, fashion, architecture, finance, publishing, and more. A great deal of what happens in New York affects what happens around the country and even around the world!

See if you can find all the things you did or didn't know about New York City in this picture. Don't forget to look for the following fun things, too!

- ☐ Airplanes (2)
- ☐ Apple
- ☐ Baseball
- ☐ Bird
- ☐ Blimp
- ☐ Book
- ☐ Boom box
- ☐ Container ship
- ☐ Diver
- ☐ Ferry
- ☐ Fish
- ☐ Flower
- ☐ Flying saucer
- ☐ Football
- ☐ Ghost
- ☐ Heart
- ☐ Helicopter
- ☐ Hot-air balloon
- ☐ King Kongs (2)
- ☐ Kite
- ☐ Parachutist
- ☐ Periscope
- ☐ Rocking chair
- ☐ Rowboat
- ☐ Star
- ☐ Telescope
- ☐ Tire
- ☐ Top hat
- ☐ Tugboat
- ☐ Worm

Who first settled New York?
When was New York C
the nation's capital?

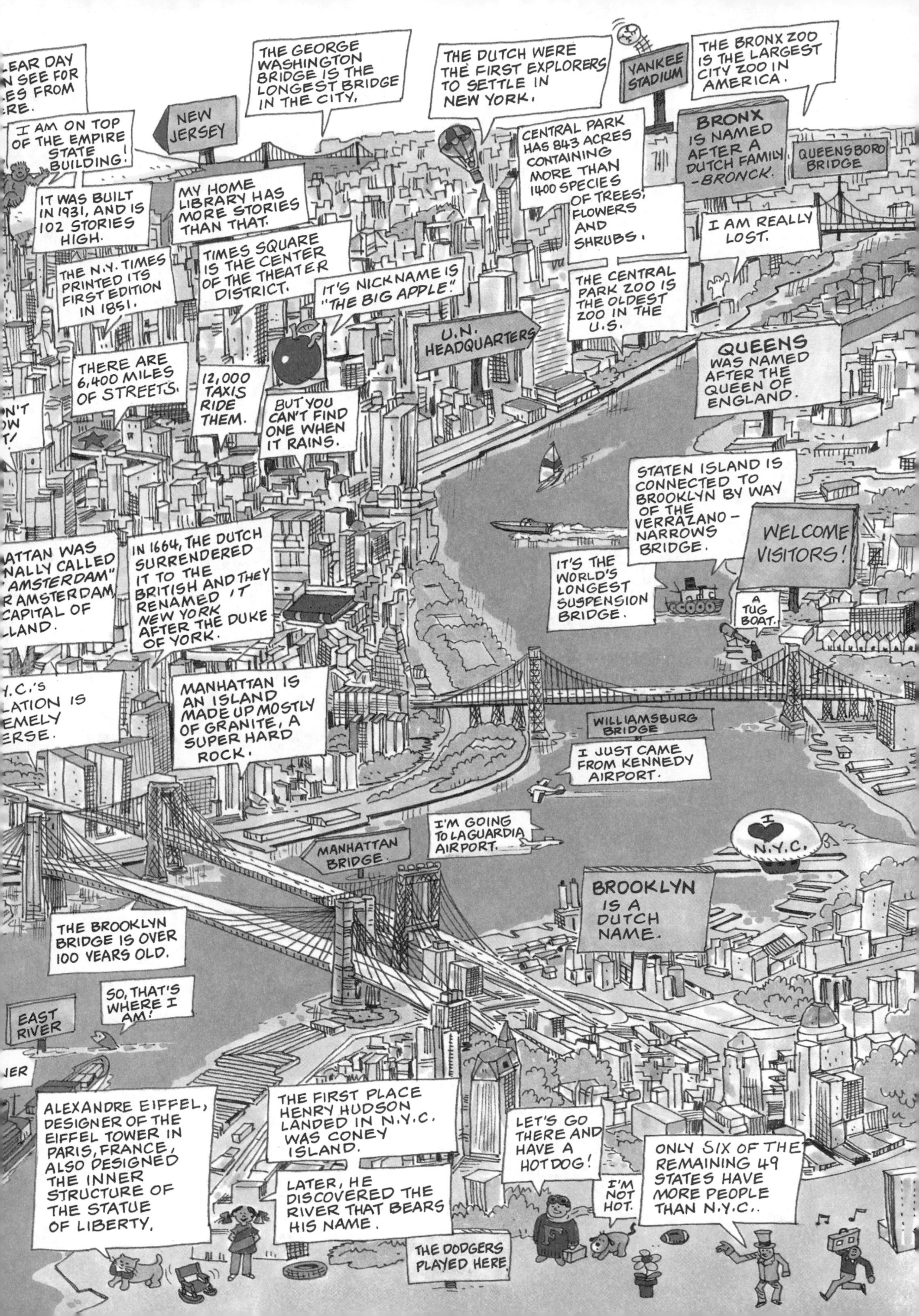

LEAR DAY N SEE FOR ES FROM RE.
THE GEORGE WASHINGTON BRIDGE IS THE LONGEST BRIDGE IN THE CITY.
THE DUTCH WERE THE FIRST EXPLORERS TO SETTLE IN NEW YORK.
YANKEE STADIUM
THE BRONX ZOO IS THE LARGEST CITY ZOO IN AMERICA.
I AM ON TOP OF THE EMPIRE STATE BUILDING!
NEW JERSEY
CENTRAL PARK HAS 843 ACRES CONTAINING MORE THAN 1400 SPECIES OF TREES, FLOWERS AND SHRUBS.
BRONX IS NAMED AFTER A DUTCH FAMILY -BRONCK.
QUEENSBORO BRIDGE
IT WAS BUILT IN 1931, AND IS 102 STORIES HIGH.
MY HOME LIBRARY HAS MORE STORIES THAN THAT.
I AM REALLY LOST.
THE N.Y. TIMES PRINTED ITS FIRST EDITION IN 1851.
TIMES SQUARE IS THE CENTER OF THE THEATER DISTRICT.
IT'S NICKNAME IS "THE BIG APPLE"
THE CENTRAL PARK ZOO IS THE OLDEST ZOO IN THE U.S.
U.N. HEADQUARTERS
THERE ARE 6,400 MILES OF STREETS.
12,000 TAXIS RIDE THEM.
BUT YOU CAN'T FIND ONE WHEN IT RAINS.
QUEENS WAS NAMED AFTER THE QUEEN OF ENGLAND.
N'T W T!
STATEN ISLAND IS CONNECTED TO BROOKLYN BY WAY OF THE VERRAZANO-NARROWS BRIDGE.
WELCOME VISITORS!
HATTAN WAS NALLY CALLED "AMSTERDAM" R AMSTERDAM, CAPITAL OF LLAND.
IN 1664, THE DUTCH SURRENDERED IT TO THE BRITISH AND THEY RENAMED IT NEW YORK AFTER THE DUKE OF YORK.
IT'S THE WORLD'S LONGEST SUSPENSION BRIDGE.
A TUG BOAT.
Y.C.'S LATION IS EMELY ERSE.
MANHATTAN IS AN ISLAND MADE UP MOSTLY OF GRANITE, A SUPER HARD ROCK.
WILLIAMSBURG BRIDGE
I JUST CAME FROM KENNEDY AIRPORT.
I'M GOING TO LAGUARDIA AIRPORT.
MANHATTAN BRIDGE
I ♥ N.Y.C.
BROOKLYN IS A DUTCH NAME.
THE BROOKLYN BRIDGE IS OVER 100 YEARS OLD.
SO, THAT'S WHERE I AM!
EAST RIVER
NER
ALEXANDRE EIFFEL, DESIGNER OF THE EIFFEL TOWER IN PARIS, FRANCE, ALSO DESIGNED THE INNER STRUCTURE OF THE STATUE OF LIBERTY.
THE FIRST PLACE HENRY HUDSON LANDED IN N.Y.C. WAS CONEY ISLAND.
LATER, HE DISCOVERED THE RIVER THAT BEARS HIS NAME.
LET'S GO THERE AND HAVE A HOT DOG!
I'M NOT HOT.
ONLY SIX OF THE REMAINING 49 STATES HAVE MORE PEOPLE THAN N.Y.C..
THE DODGERS PLAYED HERE

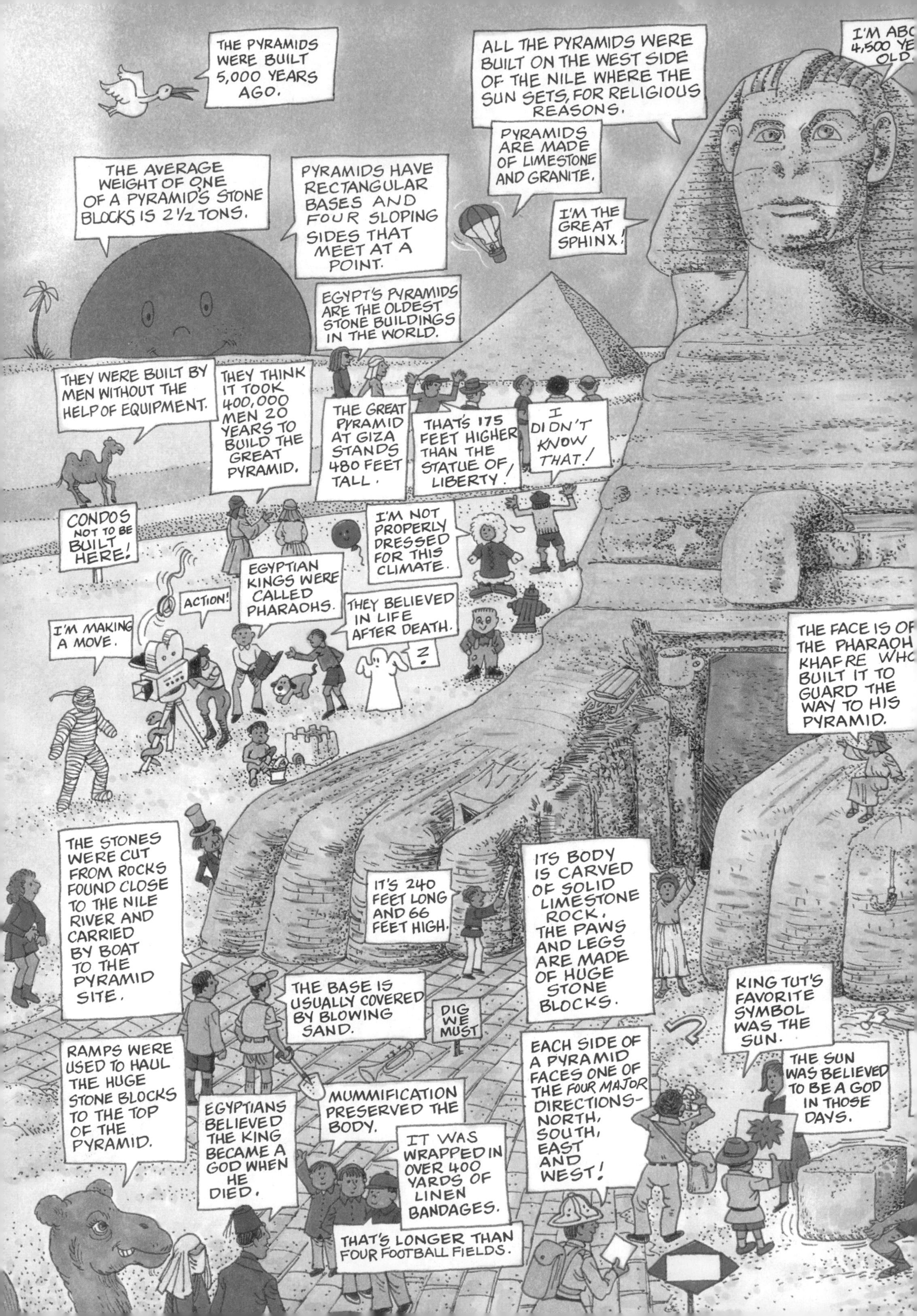
THE PYRAMIDS WERE BUILT 5,000 YEARS AGO.
ALL THE PYRAMIDS WERE BUILT ON THE WEST SIDE OF THE NILE WHERE THE SUN SETS, FOR RELIGIOUS REASONS.
I'M ABO 4,500 YE OLD.
PYRAMIDS ARE MADE OF LIMESTONE AND GRANITE.
THE AVERAGE WEIGHT OF ONE OF A PYRAMID'S STONE BLOCKS IS 2 1/2 TONS.
PYRAMIDS HAVE RECTANGULAR BASES AND FOUR SLOPING SIDES THAT MEET AT A POINT.
I'M THE GREAT SPHINX!
EGYPT'S PYRAMIDS ARE THE OLDEST STONE BUILDINGS IN THE WORLD.
THEY WERE BUILT BY MEN WITHOUT THE HELP OF EQUIPMENT.
THEY THINK IT TOOK 400,000 MEN 20 YEARS TO BUILD THE GREAT PYRAMID.
THE GREAT PYRAMID AT GIZA STANDS 480 FEET TALL.
THAT'S 175 FEET HIGHER THAN THE STATUE OF LIBERTY!
I DIDN'T KNOW THAT!
CONDOS NOT TO BE BUILT HERE!
I'M NOT PROPERLY DRESSED FOR THIS CLIMATE.
EGYPTIAN KINGS WERE CALLED PHARAOHS.
ACTION!
THEY BELIEVED IN LIFE AFTER DEATH.
I'M MAKING A MOVE.
Z
THE FACE IS OF THE PHARAOH KHAFRE WHO BUILT IT TO GUARD THE WAY TO HIS PYRAMID.
THE STONES WERE CUT FROM ROCKS FOUND CLOSE TO THE NILE RIVER AND CARRIED BY BOAT TO THE PYRAMID SITE.
IT'S 240 FEET LONG AND 66 FEET HIGH.
ITS BODY IS CARVED OF SOLID LIMESTONE ROCK. THE PAWS AND LEGS ARE MADE OF HUGE STONE BLOCKS.
THE BASE IS USUALLY COVERED BY BLOWING SAND.
DIG WE MUST
KING TUT'S FAVORITE SYMBOL WAS THE SUN.
RAMPS WERE USED TO HAUL THE HUGE STONE BLOCKS TO THE TOP OF THE PYRAMID.
EACH SIDE OF A PYRAMID FACES ONE OF THE FOUR MAJOR DIRECTIONS- NORTH, SOUTH, EAST AND WEST!
THE SUN WAS BELIEVED TO BE A GOD IN THOSE DAYS.
EGYPTIANS BELIEVED THE KING BECAME A GOD WHEN HE DIED.
MUMMIFICATION PRESERVED THE BODY.
IT WAS WRAPPED IN OVER 400 YARDS OF LINEN BANDAGES.
THAT'S LONGER THAN FOUR FOOTBALL FIELDS.

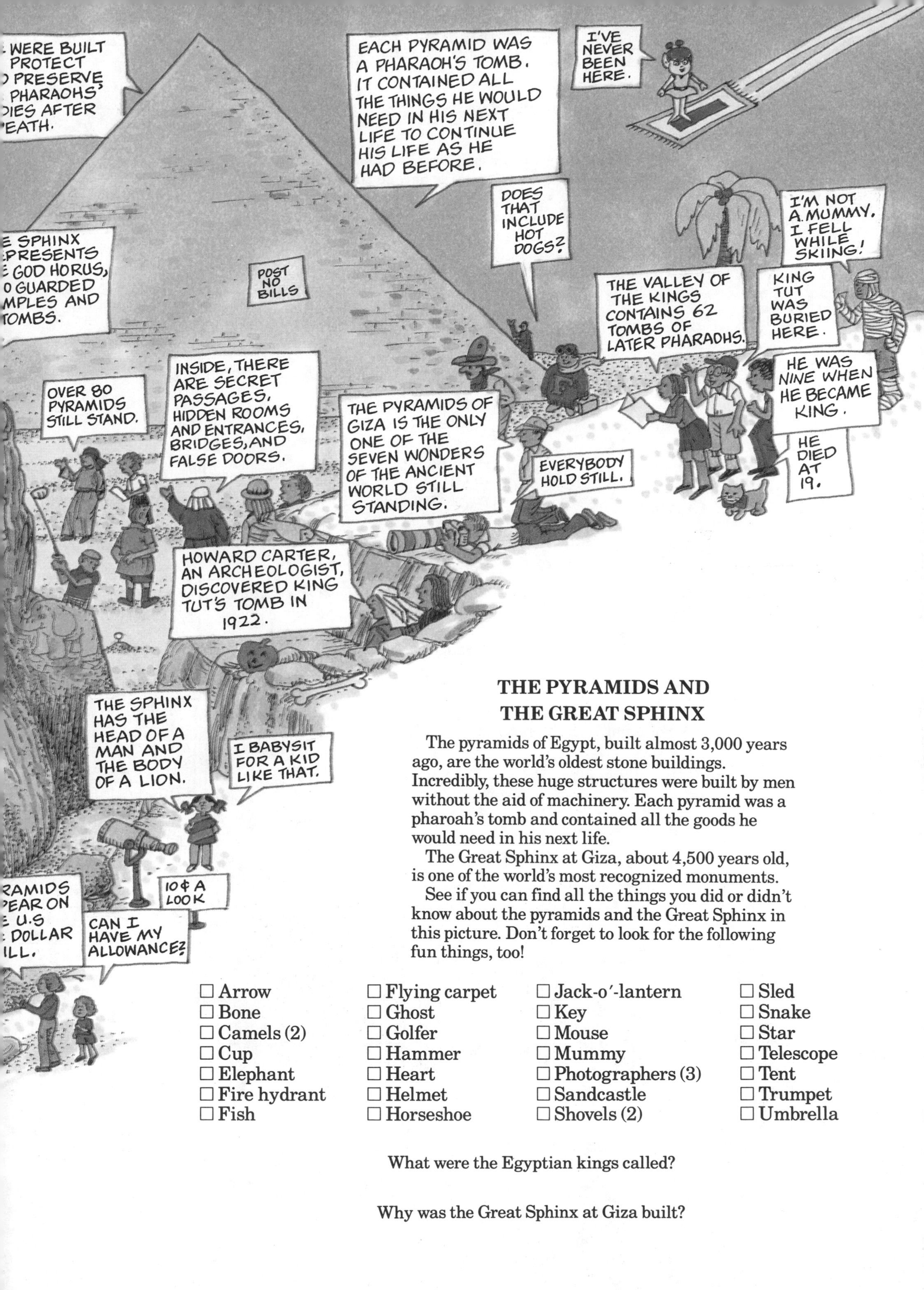

THE PYRAMIDS AND THE GREAT SPHINX

The pyramids of Egypt, built almost 3,000 years ago, are the world's oldest stone buildings. Incredibly, these huge structures were built by men without the aid of machinery. Each pyramid was a pharoah's tomb and contained all the goods he would need in his next life.

The Great Sphinx at Giza, about 4,500 years old, is one of the world's most recognized monuments.

See if you can find all the things you did or didn't know about the pyramids and the Great Sphinx in this picture. Don't forget to look for the following fun things, too!

☐ Arrow	☐ Flying carpet	☐ Jack-o'-lantern	☐ Sled
☐ Bone	☐ Ghost	☐ Key	☐ Snake
☐ Camels (2)	☐ Golfer	☐ Mouse	☐ Star
☐ Cup	☐ Hammer	☐ Mummy	☐ Telescope
☐ Elephant	☐ Heart	☐ Photographers (3)	☐ Tent
☐ Fire hydrant	☐ Helmet	☐ Sandcastle	☐ Trumpet
☐ Fish	☐ Horseshoe	☐ Shovels (2)	☐ Umbrella

What were the Egyptian kings called?

Why was the Great Sphinx at Giza built?

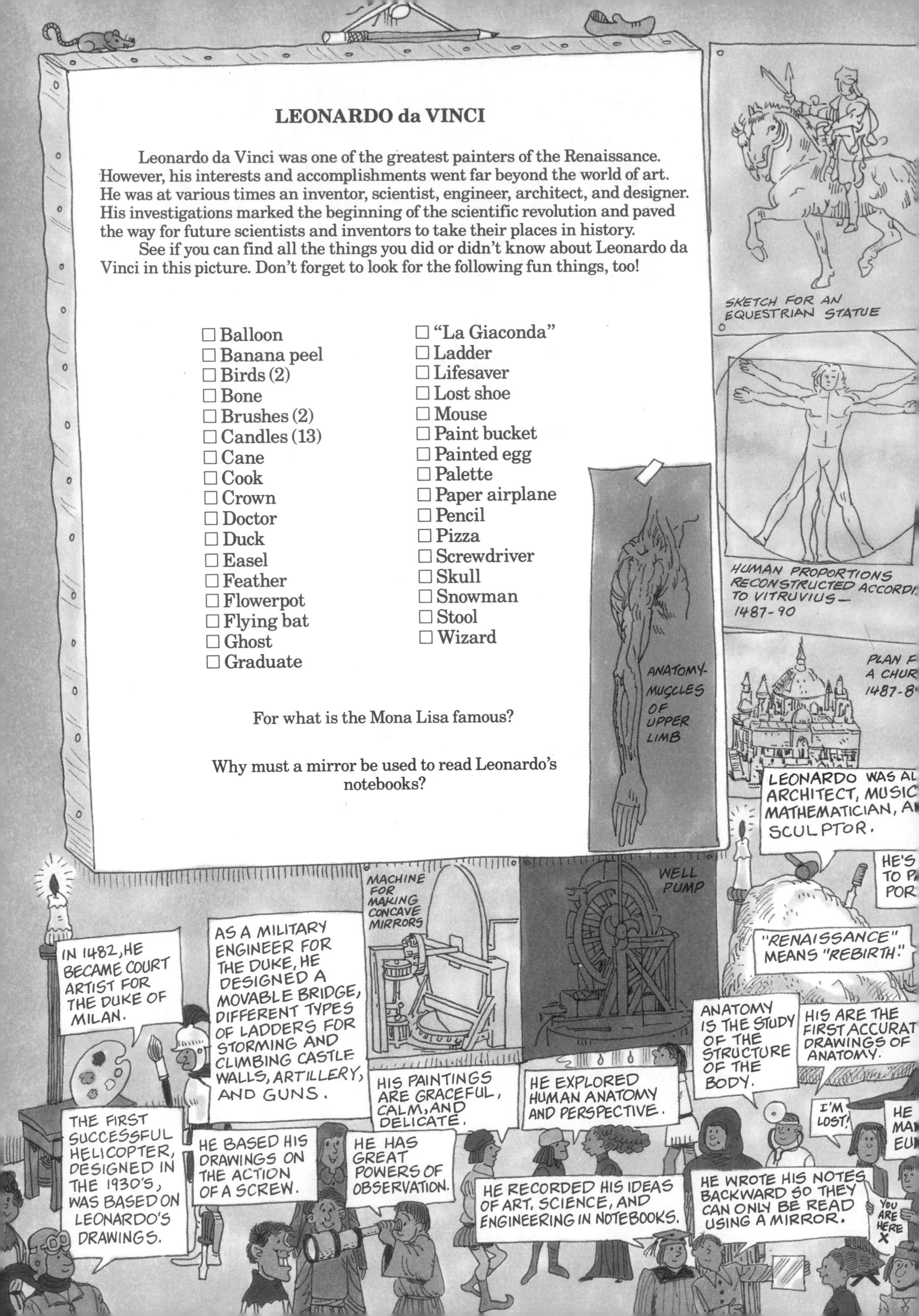

LEONARDO da VINCI

Leonardo da Vinci was one of the greatest painters of the Renaissance. However, his interests and accomplishments went far beyond the world of art. He was at various times an inventor, scientist, engineer, architect, and designer. His investigations marked the beginning of the scientific revolution and paved the way for future scientists and inventors to take their places in history.

See if you can find all the things you did or didn't know about Leonardo da Vinci in this picture. Don't forget to look for the following fun things, too!

- ☐ Balloon
- ☐ Banana peel
- ☐ Birds (2)
- ☐ Bone
- ☐ Brushes (2)
- ☐ Candles (13)
- ☐ Cane
- ☐ Cook
- ☐ Crown
- ☐ Doctor
- ☐ Duck
- ☐ Easel
- ☐ Feather
- ☐ Flowerpot
- ☐ Flying bat
- ☐ Ghost
- ☐ Graduate
- ☐ "La Giaconda"
- ☐ Ladder
- ☐ Lifesaver
- ☐ Lost shoe
- ☐ Mouse
- ☐ Paint bucket
- ☐ Painted egg
- ☐ Palette
- ☐ Paper airplane
- ☐ Pencil
- ☐ Pizza
- ☐ Screwdriver
- ☐ Skull
- ☐ Snowman
- ☐ Stool
- ☐ Wizard

For what is the Mona Lisa famous?

Why must a mirror be used to read Leonardo's notebooks?

SKETCH FOR AN EQUESTRIAN STATUE
HUMAN PROPORTIONS RECONSTRUCTED ACCORDI TO VITRUVIUS— 1487-90
ANATOMY- MUSCLES OF UPPER LIMB
MACHINE FOR MAKING CONCAVE MIRRORS
WELL PUMP
"RENAISSANCE" MEANS "REBIRTH."
IN 1482, HE BECAME COURT ARTIST FOR THE DUKE OF MILAN.
AS A MILITARY ENGINEER FOR THE DUKE, HE DESIGNED A MOVABLE BRIDGE, DIFFERENT TYPES OF LADDERS FOR STORMING AND CLIMBING CASTLE WALLS, ARTILLERY, AND GUNS.
HIS PAINTINGS ARE GRACEFUL, CALM, AND DELICATE.
HE EXPLORED HUMAN ANATOMY AND PERSPECTIVE.
ANATOMY IS THE STUDY OF THE STRUCTURE OF THE BODY.
THE FIRST SUCCESSFUL HELICOPTER, DESIGNED IN THE 1930'S, WAS BASED ON LEONARDO'S DRAWINGS.
HE BASED HIS DRAWINGS ON THE ACTION OF A SCREW.
HE HAS GREAT POWERS OF OBSERVATION.
HE RECORDED HIS IDEAS OF ART, SCIENCE, AND ENGINEERING IN NOTEBOOKS.
HE WROTE HIS NOTES BACKWARD SO THEY CAN ONLY BE READ USING A MIRROR.
I'M LOST!
YOU ARE HERE X

I'M TESTING HIS FLYING MACHINE.
THAT LOOKS LIKE MY SPACESHIP.
LOOK OUT BELOW!
I'M ABOUT TO GO OUT!
ARMORED CAR – 1485
MORTAR TO HURL STONES
HE'S GOING TO FALL AND BREAK A LEG!
HE INVENTED THE PARACHUTE.
DON'T SHOOT!
HE INVENTED THE TURNSPIT FOR ROASTING MEAT.
MACHINE GUN
HELICOPTER
HE MADE A SCREW-CUTTING MACHINE WHICH WAS USED UNTIL THE 1900'S.
HE CHANGED FROM AN ARTIST-INVENTOR INTO A SCIENTIST.
Z
X-RAYS WERE TAKEN OF THE MONA LISA. UNDERNEATH THE FINAL MASTERPIECE, LEONARDO PAINTED THREE COMPLETELY DIFFERENT VERSIONS OF THE SAME WOMAN.
I HAVE TO PAINT "THE LAST SUPPER" ON A MONASTERY WALL BETWEEN 1495-97.
THE MONA LISA HAS NO EYEBROWS!
IT WAS FASHIONABLE IN RENAISSANCE FLORENCE TO SHAVE THEM OFF.
I MAKE PEOPLE SMILE.
THE PAINTING IS FAMOUS FOR HER MYSTERIOUS SMILE.
IT WAS BOMBED DURING W.W. II. DAMPNESS HAS DAMAGED IT.
ANOTHER TOUR THROUGH MY STUDIO!
DRAW ME.
NAPOLEON'S SOLDIERS USED "THE LAST SUPPER" FOR TARGET PRACTICE!
IT ONLY MEASURES 24 BY 24 INCHES.
FOR RENT
HE WAS BORN IN VINCI, NEAR FLORENCE, ITALY IN 1452.
HE INVENTED THE SCISSORS.
HE INVENTED THE BICYCLE, 300 YEARS BEFORE IT APPEARED ON THE ROAD.
THAT'S WHY HE BECAME A VEGETARIAN.
NICE PICTURE.
HE CREATED AN INFLATABLE TUBE SO THAT PEOPLE COULD FLOAT IN WATER.
HE WAS TRAINED TO BE A PAINTER.
HE DESIGNED A DIVING SUIT.
HE DESIGNED A REVOLVING STAGE FOR PLAYS AND PAGEANTS.

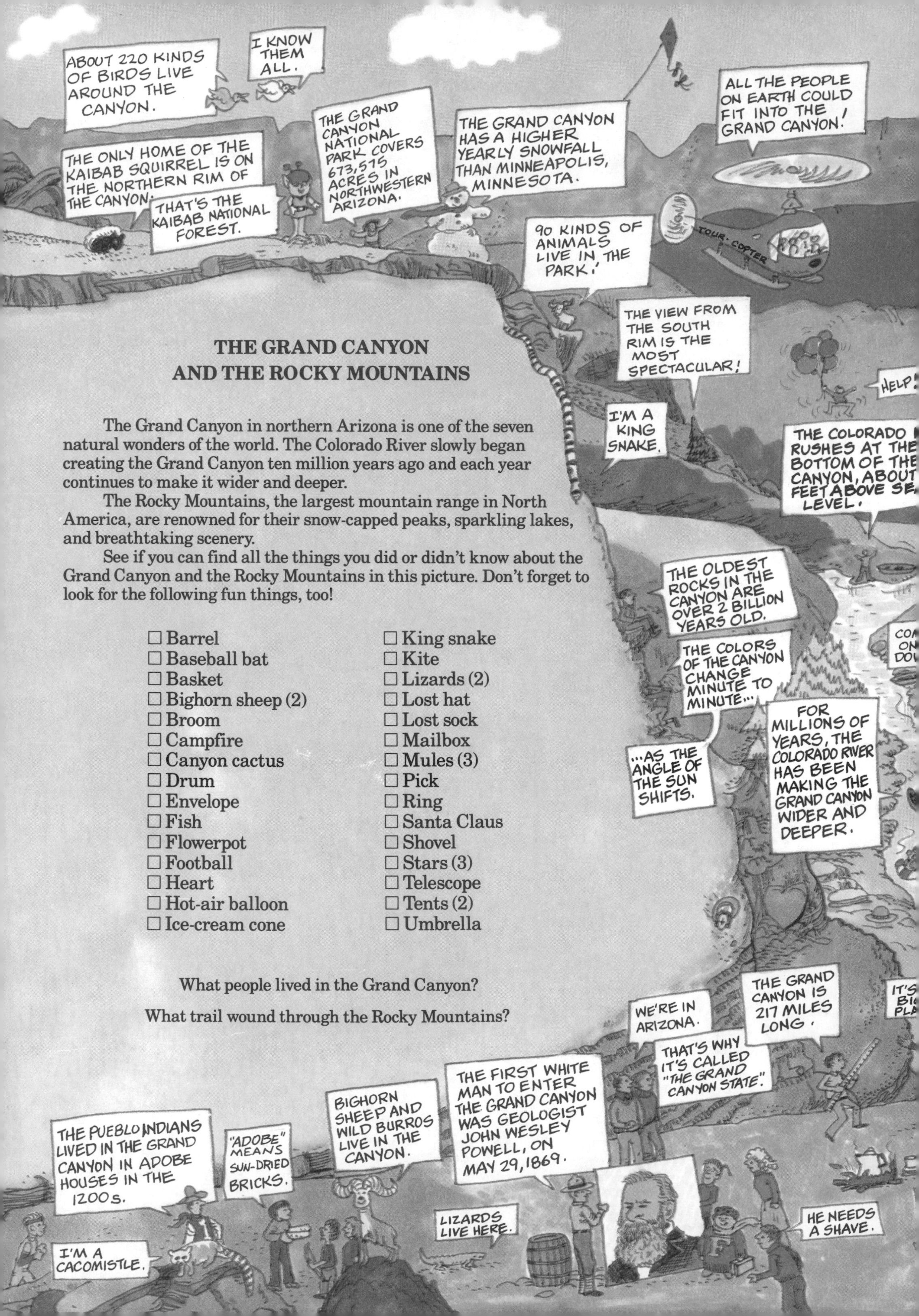

THE GRAND CANYON AND THE ROCKY MOUNTAINS

The Grand Canyon in northern Arizona is one of the seven natural wonders of the world. The Colorado River slowly began creating the Grand Canyon ten million years ago and each year continues to make it wider and deeper.

The Rocky Mountains, the largest mountain range in North America, are renowned for their snow-capped peaks, sparkling lakes, and breathtaking scenery.

See if you can find all the things you did or didn't know about the Grand Canyon and the Rocky Mountains in this picture. Don't forget to look for the following fun things, too!

- ☐ Barrel
- ☐ Baseball bat
- ☐ Basket
- ☐ Bighorn sheep (2)
- ☐ Broom
- ☐ Campfire
- ☐ Canyon cactus
- ☐ Drum
- ☐ Envelope
- ☐ Fish
- ☐ Flowerpot
- ☐ Football
- ☐ Heart
- ☐ Hot-air balloon
- ☐ Ice-cream cone
- ☐ King snake
- ☐ Kite
- ☐ Lizards (2)
- ☐ Lost hat
- ☐ Lost sock
- ☐ Mailbox
- ☐ Mules (3)
- ☐ Pick
- ☐ Ring
- ☐ Santa Claus
- ☐ Shovel
- ☐ Stars (3)
- ☐ Telescope
- ☐ Tents (2)
- ☐ Umbrella

What people lived in the Grand Canyon?

What trail wound through the Rocky Mountains?

YOU'RE LITTERING THE PARK BY DOING THAT!
FORESTS GROW NEAR AND ALONG THE RIMS.
A TRAIL THROUGH THE CANYON CONNECTS BOTH RIMS.
THE CANYON'S SIDES ARE MADE UP OF CLIFFS, HILLS, ROCKS, RIDGES, AND VALLEYS.
THE FIRST EUROPEANS TO REACH THE ROCKIES WERE SPANISH EXPLORERS.
THEY STARTED A COLONY NEAR SANTA FE, NEW MEXICO.
FOR RENT
WHICH WAY
ME
N FROM
ERE!
IN SOME PLACES IT IS NOW 18 MILES ACROSS AND ONE MILE DEEP... THAT'S A LOT OF CANYON!
THE NORTH RIM OF THE CANYON IS ABOUT 1200 FEET HIGHER THAN THE SOUTH RIM.
IN 1805-06, LEWIS AND CLARK TRAVELED THROUGH THE NORTHERN ROCKIES.
BOY, AM I LOST!
THE ROCKY MOUNTAINS ARE ABOUT 70 MILLION YEARS OLD.
THIS IS A VERY BEAUTIFUL SIGHT!
YES, AND I FORGOT TO BRING MY CAMERA!
THE CANYON IS ONE OF THE SEVEN NATURAL WONDERS OF THE WORLD.
I'M LATE!
IT'S THE LARGEST MOUNTAIN SYSTEM IN NORTH AMERICA.
THE GRAND CANYON BECAME A NATIONAL PARK IN 1919.
YOU CAN HIKE INTO THE CANYON OR RIDE MULES DOWN AND BACK.
WHY DON'T YOU HIKE?
THE OREGON TRAIL, THE LONGEST OVERLAND ROUTE USED BY EXPLORERS, WOUND THROUGH THE ROCKIES.
HE COLORADO
IVER BEGAN
REATING THE
RAND
ANYON 10
ILLION YEARS AGO.
IT WORE AWAY (ERODED) ABOUT ONE INCH PER CENTURY.
A CENTURY IS 100 YEARS.
I'M AN AVOCET.
KEEP THE CANYON CLEAN!
I'M A COUGAR AND YOU'RE NOT.
I'M A MULE DEER
DON'T SIT ON ME!
ORADO, RIO GRANDE,
AS, MISSOURI,
OLUMBIA RIVERS
EGIN IN THE
KIES!
I'M SITTING THIS ONE OUT.
FROM NORTHERN ALASKA TO NORTHERN NEW MEXICO.
THE ROCKY MOUNTAINS EXTEND FOR MORE THAN 3,000 MILES ACROSS THE WESTERN PART OF NORTH AMERICA.
YELLOWSTONE NATIONAL PARK— HOME OF THE GEYSER "OLD FAITHFUL"
CANADA
U.S.A.
ROCKY MOUNTAINS
WASH.
MONTANA
ORE.
WYOMING
IDAHO
NEVADA
PIKE'S PEAK
UTAH
COLORADO
GRAND CANYON
CALIF.
ARIZONA
NEW MEXICO

CHRISTOPHER COLUMBUS

Christopher Columbus was one of the greatest explorers of all time. In 1492, he left Spain and set sail for Asia with his three ships, the Nina, the Pinta, and the Santa Maria. Columbus never made it to the East Indies. Instead, he discovered the New World which is known today as the Americas.

See if you can find all the things you did or didn't know about Christopher Columbus. Don't forget to look for the following fun things, too!

- ☐ Arrows (2)
- ☐ Barrel
- ☐ Basket
- ☐ Bone
- ☐ Duck
- ☐ Egg
- ☐ Fish (4)
- ☐ Flower
- ☐ Hummingbird
- ☐ Jack-o'-lantern
- ☐ Key
- ☐ Laundry
- ☐ Moustache
- ☐ Octopus
- ☐ Parrot
- ☐ Periscope
- ☐ Pig
- ☐ Sea serpent
- ☐ Sick sailor
- ☐ Snake
- ☐ Spaceship
- ☐ Spears
- ☐ Sword
- ☐ T-shirt
- ☐ Telescope
- ☐ Tire
- ☐ Turtle
- ☐ Wooden leg

Who helped finance the trip?

How many voyages did Columbus make?

COLUMBUS WAS NEVER OUT TO PROVE THE WORLD WAS ROUND.
WAS JUST LOOKING
R THE SHORTEST
UTE TO THE SPICE
LANDS IN ASIA.
THE PINTA HAS 26 MEN.
THE NINA HAS ONLY 24 MEN.
HI, MOM!
WE HAVE 40 MEN ON BOARD.
WE'LL COME BACK IN ABOUT 500 YEARS.
THEY'LL PROBABLY HAVE A PARTY, THEN.
OOPS!
THERE IS NO SUCH THING AS ME!
I HOPE I'M ON ALL FOUR VOYAGES.
WE SAILED WEST FROM PALOS, SPAIN ON AUGUST 3, 1492.
WE'RE ON THE SANTA MARIA!
IT'S COLUMBUS'S FLAGSHIP.
THE EAST INDIES ARE WHERE SILK AND SPICES COME FROM.
I'M SEASICK.
EDGE OF WORLD
WEST
EAST
MAN OVERBOARD!
I'M HERE TOO.
PORTUGAL'S RULERS TURNED HIM DOWN ON HIS PLAN TO SAIL TO THE EAST INDIES.
TODAY IS OCTOBER 12, 1492.
WE'RE IN THE BAHAMAS.
THIS MUST BE SAN SALVADOR ISLAND.
ARCO
OLO
VAS
IS
ERO!
I CLAIM THIS LAND FOR SPAIN!
I WANT TO GO HOME!
I FORGOT MY SUIT!
OUCH! MY FOOT!
WE MADE IT!
EL JUNK
VERY QUICK SAND!
YOUR
YOU ARE HERE
18
NO LITTERING
I THOUGHT COLUMBUS WAS LIKE A SCHOOL BUS.
EN ISABELLA OF
IN HELPED FINANCE
UMBUS'S TRIP
E.
TOO BAD! SHE SHOULD HAVE SPENT THE MONEY ON TACO STANDS.
I WONDER IF THE THREE SHIPS WILL MAKE IT BACK TO SPAIN.
I LOVE BUBBLE GUM!
FREDDIE IS THE BEST LOOKING ONE!
WHICH ONE IS FREDDIE?
THEY SHOULD ARRIVE IN SPAIN SOMETIME NEXT MARCH.
DO YOU HAVE FRENCH FRIES?
YOU CAN'T! IT HASN'T BEEN INVENTED YET!!
YAMS FOR SALE
NICE PICTURE.
IF I CAN'T SELL THEM, I'LL EAT THEM!!
HIRED A BAND.
IF I KNEW THEY WERE COMING I'D HAVE BAKED A CAKE.